Solomon Northup's
Twelve Years a Slave
1841-1853

Rewritten for Young Readers
by SUE EAKIN

PELICAN PUBLISHING COMPANY
Gretna 1998

Published by The Everett Companies, 1989
Published by arrangement with the author by
    Pelican Publishing Company, Inc., 1998

First Pelican edition, September 1998

Library of Congress Cataloging-in-Publication Data

Eakin, Sue L.
    Solomon Northup's Twelve years a slave : 1841-1853 / rewritten for
young readers by Sue Eakin.—1st Pelican ed.
    Summary: Describes the life of Solomon Northup, a free Black man
from Saratoga, N.Y., who was kidnapped in 1841 and forced into slavery
in Louisiana for twelve years.
    ISBN 1-56554-344-0 (pbk. : alk. paper)
    1. Northup, Solomon, b. 1808—Juvenile literature. 2. Slaves—United
States—Biography—Juvenile literature. 3. Slaves' writings, American—
Juvenile literature. 4. Afro-Americans—Biography—Juvenile literature.
5. Plantation life—Louisiana—History—19th century—Juvenile literature. 6. Slavery—Louisiana—History—19th century—Juvenile literature. [1. Northup, Solomon, b. 1808. 2. Slaves. 3. Afro-Americans—
Biography. 4. Slavery—Louisiana.] I. Northup, Solomon, b. 1808. Twelve
years a slave. II. Title.
E444.N87 1998
976.3'05'092—dc21
[B]   98-29404
                                                                        CIP
                                                                         AC

Manufactured in the United States of America

Published by Pelican Publishing Company, Inc.
1000 Burmaster Street, Gretna, Louisiana 70053

DEDICATED

to

Ninoska Eakin
Gretchen Kuhn
Sarah Lyles
and
Amy Uffman

TO THE READER:

This true story of a slave, Solomon Northup, has been described as the best firsthand account of slavery in existence. The original book has been rewritten for young readers, but the exact words of Solomon Northup have been used as much as possible. Solomon Northup used words, such as "nigger," that would not be acceptable today. These words have been used in the young readers' version in the exact locations in which they were used in the original account by Northup himself. Certain names, like Chafin, Windes, and Tibaut, are spelled differently from the original text. Northup had never seen these words written down and so spelled them the way they sounded to him. The spelling was different from that found in the U. S. Census.

The idea has been to preserve the story and spirit of those times in the words of one who was there. That way young readers will learn to think and make judgments about the period from an actual slave experience.

Language, like customs, and laws, and outlooks of people change over the years. This is history: the story of the way it was during Solomon Northup's twelve years in slavery, 1841-1853, as told by Solomon himself.

Illustrations Especially
Designed by
P.A. ("PAP") DEAN, JR.

TABLE OF CONTENTS

CHAPTER ONE

This story began in the State of New York in 1841. It concerns the Northup family, a family not much different from a number of others who lived in the resort city of Saratoga Springs.

Visitors poured into Saratoga Springs during spring and summer to bathe in the springs and to attend the horse races for which Saratoga was famous. In the city large hotels accommodated the visitors, most of whom arrived by train. Since the train depot was situated some distance from the hotels, a business had grown up for transporting guests to and from the hotels. It was a lively business with drivers of carriages, hacks, and horse-drawn buggies competing for customers.

During the tourist season, Solomon Northup, a man part white and part black, drove one of the hacks. Since he was part black himself, Solomon was very mindful of the existence of slavery in the United States. There were no slaves in New York, but there were slaves in some of the other Northern states. Most slaves lived in the agricultural South. Both Solomon's parents were Free People of Color, so Solomon was born free. His wife, Anne, was also free.

When our story begins, Saratoga was waiting for the tourist season to open. Northup, like the other hack drivers, now was unemployed. During the busy season both he and Anne worked for the United States Hotel, one of the most popular in the city. While he drove a hack for the hotel, Anne was a cook.

Fig. 1. Solomon liked to walk with his children: Elizabeth, age 10; Margaret, age 8; and Alonzo, 5.

Fig. 2. When he was not working, Solomon Northup liked to play the fiddle. Anne and his children liked to hear him play.

When she was not employed there, it was her habit to go to Sandy Hill, about twenty miles away, and work as a cook at Sherrill's Coffee House. She was there at this time and had taken their oldest child, Elizabeth, 10, with her. The other two children, Margaret, 8, and Alonzo, 5, were staying with their aunt in Saratoga while their mother was away at her job.

Over the years Solomon Northup had worked at many kinds of jobs during the winter seasons. Once he had taken a job rafting logs on Lake Champlain, hiring workers to assist him in the job. During one such employment, he had visited Canada, going into the City of Montreal and out into the surrounding towns and rural areas. He had worked as a carpenter and at various other odd jobs until the tourist season opened again. Always, he had had his violin, or fiddle, as some called it, to depend upon since he was in demand to play for dances and different occasions. That way he earned money for his family until he started driving the hack for the hotel again.

CHAPTER TWO

With all his family away from home, Northup was alone. One day in March, 1841, before the resort season opened, Northup was walking downtown with hopes he might find somebody who needed a person to work. He decided to stop by a tavern where men were sitting around talking. Not long after he joined them, two strangers came up to him and introduced themselves. The men said their names were Merrill Brown and Abram Hamilton. They were very friendly.

They told Northup that they belonged to a circus company, which was then in Washington, D. C., waiting for spring when the circus traveled, presenting entertainment from city to city. Meantime, they were enjoying touring the countryside. To pay for their expenses they had a juggling act that they were presenting at night. They told him they had had much trouble securing music for their entertainments. When Northup told them he played the fiddle, they seemed excited. They told Northup if he would travel with them, they would pay him a dollar a day and three dollars per night for each night he played for their performances. This, Solomon figured, would allow ample funds for his return trip to Saratoga.

Their offer sounded fine to Northup, and he decided to accept it. They were in a hurry, they said, so he rushed home to get his fiddle. In a hurry to return to his new employers, he did not leave a note for Anne about the new job. He figured he would be

Fig. 3. **Soon Solomon was riding with the two men in a fine carriage.**

back in Saratoga before she returned home. The men were pleased he was going with them.

Soon he found himself serving as the driver of their fine covered carriage drawn by two handsome horses. Behind him sat the friendly strangers.

Merrill Brown and Abram Hamilton were both heavily bearded and wore their hair long. Brown appeared to be about forty years old and was short and heavy. He wore a black frock coat and black hat. Hamilton was younger, probably about twenty-five years old, Northup estimated, and the more worldly of the two. He was tall and slender and very fashionably dressed with a snuff-colored coat, a glossy hat, and a fancy vest.

Northup loved to perform with his fiddle, and he enjoyed the first night's performance. It turned out to be the only performance of the trip. The next day Brown and Hamilton spoke of the necessity of joining the circus without delay, so they drove on, not stopping for further programs. When they reached New York City, which was to be the end of his journey with them, the men urged Solomon to continue with them to Washington City. They told him that he would receive high wages and that the circus soon would be headed North. With such promises Northup finally decided the opportunity was too good to miss and decided to remain with them.

Before leaving New York the next morning they told Solomon he should go to the courthouse and obtain papers proving he was a free man. They told him that, although New York was a free state, they were going into a slave state, and he would need such papers. Northup thought this was probably a good idea, and together the trio went to the customhouse. Brown and Hamilton swore before the clerk that Northup was a free man. Papers attesting to the fact that he was free were prepared and handed to Northup. He stuck the papers in his pocket, not having the faintest idea he would have need of them.

The tension Hamilton and Brown seemed to be under increased as the carriage crossed into Pennsylvania, heading for Philadelphia. They spent the night there before continuing the next morning into Baltimore, Maryland. Finally they arrived at their destination — Washington, D. C.

It was a day of great excitement in the capital. The President of the United States was dead, and his funeral was to be held the next day. William H. Harrison had only been president a few weeks. He had spoken for an hour in a cold rain at his inauguration. Later he became ill and died.

The next day Solomon stood with his new friends watching the funeral procession of President Harrison coming slowly down the avenue. It was a long procession of carriages followed by thousands of people walking slowly on foot to the melancholy funeral dirge. Bells tolled and cannon shot filled the air. Hamilton and Brown walked to the capitol afterwards and strolled across the grounds. Northup walked with them while his new friends pointed out places of interest here and there. Despite their earlier rush to return to the circus, there was no mention of it.

Fig. 4. *In Washington, D. C., the two men with whom he was traveling gave Solomon a drink which made him violently ill.*

Several times during the day Brown and Hamilton stopped by taverns and purchased whiskey, serving themselves and always pouring a glass for Northup. They were not drinking to excess, however. In the evening Brown and Hamilton took him to a saloon and sat down at a table to drink. They bought liquor and poured whiskey for Solomon. After one glass of the liquid, Northup suddenly became very ill. He suffered a bad headache and became sick at his stomach.

At supper he wanted nothing to eat, and soon afterwards the servant who had shown him to a room in the hotel the night before showed him back to his room. Hamilton and Brown urged him to retire and rest.

Northup found it impossible to sleep. His head hurt so badly the pain was almost unbearable, and his lips were so dry they were parched. He wanted water, but, as soon as he finished drinking, a nightmarish thirst was there again. He was in agony. At some point he vaguely realized there were people who came into his room. Whether Hamilton and Brown were there, he did not know. Solomon was told he must get to a doctor. Men appeared beside him to help him to walk. After that he lost consciousness.

It may have been days later when Solomon finally returned to consciousness. He felt very weak. He was sitting in a very dark place on a low bench made of rough boards. He was handcuffed, and there were chains binding his ankles. He tried to stand, but he could not. There was not a sound except that of the chains when he tried to move. He tried to call for help, but there was nobody to hear. He managed to feel in his pockets and realized that both his money and his free papers were gone. Once a horrible thought came to him, "I have been kidnapped!" He dismissed it quickly and felt sure there had simply been some terrible mistake.

Fig. 5.   James J. Birch and Radburn finally opened the door to the dungeon where Northup was in chains.

CHAPTER THREE

Not a ray of light was permitted into the dungeon where Northup sat in misery. After hours in the dank, dark place, Northup heard a rooster crowing, heralding the dawn of a new day. Some time after that he could hear the distant rumble of carriages hurrying along the streets. An hour or so later he heard footsteps overhead that continued for an hour or more. Then a key was rattled in the lock of the heavy door that closed his prison. When the door swung back, a burst of sunlight came through the darkness, and two men stood in front of him. One was a powerful, gross-looking man, whose very appearance was ugly and repelling. This was James H. Birch, who, Northup learned later, was a well-known slave dealer in Washington, D. C. The other man was Birch's flunkey, Ebenezer Radburn. Radburn held the great bunch of keys with which he had unlocked the door.

"Well, Boy, how do you feel now?" Birch asked in a loud voice, looking down at Solomon. (All male slaves were called "boys." It did not matter how old the man was; he was a "Boy.")

"I am sick, and I don't know why I am here," Solomon answered.

Birch fairly hissed. "You are my slave. I bought you. I'm fixing to send you to New Orleans."

In shock, Solomon spoke up loudly. "I am a free man. I live in Saratoga, and I have a wife and three children. My name is Northup. Nobody has a right to chain me here. When I get out of here, I'm going to the law."

"You ain't going to do nothing," Birch assured him with an oath. "You are a slave, and you belong to me."

"I don't belong to no man," Solomon fairly screamed back at Birch. "Get these chains off of me!"

"Shut up!" Birch ordered with loud curses. "You are a runaway from Georgia, do you hear me?"

"Those scoundrels, Brown and Hamilton, are going to pay for this! And I'll show you whether I'm a slave or not—!" Northup countered angrily, refusing to be quiet. "I am a free man. I am a citizen of New York, and I have my rights same as you!"

Birch yelled curses at Solomon. "You black liar! You are a runaway from Georgia. That's what you are!" He turned to the man beside him. "Get me that paddle and cat-o-nine-tails. I'll show this black liar who he belongs to."

Radburn left to bring in the whips. This was the kind of work for which Radburn was paid: receiving slaves, feeding, and whipping slaves. The two men undressed Solomon and laid him face downward over the bench.

Radburn placed his foot on the chain tied between Solomon's wrists. In such a position Northup could not move. Birch took the heavy paddle through which holes had been drilled. On the paddle was tied a rope woven with leather strands from which hung thin strips of the leather. With this Birch beat the naked man mercilessly. Over and over he asked brutally if he still thought he was a free man, and

Northup's stubborn refusal to deny his freedom maddened Birch, his tormentor, to insanity.

Despite the horrible suffering, Solomon kept answering, "I am a free man!"

With every such reply Birch beat him harder than ever. He broke the wooden paddle and seized the rope, lashing Solomon's raw skin. Knots in the rope dug deep into the flesh, and Northup thought he would surely die.

Finally, no sound came from Northup. He could speak no more.

Radburn said to Birch this was surely enough. Birch finally decided to quit, shaking his fist toward Northup's face and vowing this was only a sample of what he was going to get if he ever said he was free, or kidnapped, again.

The men closed the shutter over the one small window in the room. Going out, they locked the big door.

Solomon was on fire with pain, the flesh cut and bleeding across his back and legs. Sometime later Solomon heard the key in the lock again, and his heart filled with fear. This time it was Radburn. He brought a tin plate with a slice of bread and a piece of fried pork. There was a glass of water. "Don't say nothin' no more," he tried to advise Solomon. "That'll only make things worse for you."

Radburn opened the shutter over the small window and let in a little light. He unlocked the chains around Solomon's ankles, and left Solomon alone again.

Solomon's body was sore and stiff with large blisters covering parts of his body. There was no bed, pillow, or blanket — only the damp floor on which to sleep.

The thought struck him that he had been kidnapped and sold into slavery. This was too horrible a thought to accept. He dismissed the idea quickly. He could not believe he would remain a slave. He could not believe that Brown and Hamilton, as kindly as they had treated him, had kidnapped him and sold him into slavery. He even half expected that they might come to free him at any moment. He thought surely his family would find him and force Birch to recognize the truth. He felt that Birch would not dare hold him when he found out that he was holding a free citizen of New York.

Twice a day Radburn returned with a strip of fried pork, a slice of bread, and a glass of water. The food was always the same. After several days in the lonely room, the big door was flung open. Now Solomon could go out into the yard. After being in the musty dungeon, he could scarcely see when he first walked outside. The fenced slave yard was not very large, but he could exercise his sore legs a little. He found three other slaves there — two men and a boy. He lost no time getting acquainted with them.

Clemens Ray, one of the men, had been bought by Birch. He had driven a hack and had also worked at a livery stable. Birch had told Clemens he was sending him to New Orleans to be sold on the slave market there, and the man was very distressed about that. Clemens told Solomon that this place they were in was

Williams' Slave Pen, a place of which Northup had never heard.

John Williams was the other young man. He was from Virginia. Birch had taken him on a debt his master owed the slave dealer. John Williams lived in hopes his master would come reclaim him. This did, indeed, happen.

The other slave was a child. A boy named Randall, about ten years old, sometimes played about in the yard of the slave pen. Sometimes he cried, calling for his mother and wondering when she might come to see him. He couldn't understand why she did not come.

Solomon remained about two weeks in the slave pen.

The night before he left a young woman was brought to the slave pen leading a little girl about eight years old by the hand. As soon as Randall saw them, he rushed to them, clinging to the woman's dress, and kissing the little girl over and over. They were Randall's mother and half-sister. His mother hugged him close, kissing him and speaking loving words to him. Emily, the little girl, was more than pretty; she was an extraordinarily beautiful child with long curls falling around her neck. She had big brown eyes in an oval face. Her complexion was a faultless soft tan.

Solomon was puzzled about the woman and children, even shocked that they should be here in the slave pen. They had none of the appearance of slaves. Instead, they had the appearance of people far above the ordinary financial status of most of the population. Their behavior bespoke an education and

Fig. 6.   Eliza with her two children cried all night long, and Solmon was helpless to comfort her.

refinements completely separated from that of slaves. The mother held the children close to her and never quit crying.

Solomon became very upset listening to her cry and watching the distress of the boy and girl. The children, nestled close to their mother, finally drifted off to sleep with their heads on her lap. That did not hush the mother's tears. "What will become of them! Soon they will have no mother. God knows," she cried, "I can't live if they are taken from me! I may never see them again!"

Solomon could hardly stand listening to her. He forgot his own troubles and tried to show his sympathy. After awhile he asked her name. She stopped sobbing long enough to tell him that her name was Eliza. As time passed during the night, Eliza recounted the events which had brought her and the children to William's Slave Pen. Little Emily's father was Elisha Berry, a rich white man. She, Eliza, was born on his plantation. When Eliza was a young woman, Elisha Berry left his wife and daughter in the Big House and took the slave girl, Eliza, to another plantation where he had compelled her to live with him. Emily was Elisha Berry's child. During the nine years she had lived with him, Elisha Berry had been very good to her and the children. They had lived with every comfort and had servants to attend them.

Mrs. Berry and her daughter, a Mrs. Brooks, hated Eliza and little Emily with a passion. Somehow, beyond the power of Elisha Berry to prevent, the daughter had gained legal control of the slave property. The sight of Eliza sickened Mrs. Brooks, and she could not bear to see Emily, her half-sister. The fact that Emily was uncommonly beautiful fed the woman's hate. She had her husband, Jacob Brooks, call upon Eliza on the pretense he was taking her to the city to execute her freedom papers. Therefore, she dressed herself and the child in their best clothes and had happily gone with him into Washington. There Brooks delivered them to the trader, Birch, at William's Slave Pen. The paper that was executed was the bill of sale into slavery.

CHAPTER FOUR

Eliza wept day and night.

About midnight, after Eliza and Emily were brought to the slave pen, the door to where the slaves were kept was opened. Suddenly the brute, Birch, and his hired help, Radburn, stood there with lanterns in their hands. Birch with an oath ordered the slaves to roll up their blankets and get ready to board the boat. Birch gave a rough shake to the children to wake them. Everybody must hurry, he ordered with another oath.

Solomon and Clem were handcuffed together and ordered to march at the head of the line of slaves. With their free hands, Solomon and Clem were told to take the handles of a trunk belonging to Birch and lead the way. Eliza and the children followed.

It was a dark night. Not even a straggler could be seen on the streets. Everything was quiet. Radburn, holding a stick, marched behind the slaves, prodding the sleeping children to hurry along. Northup could see the capital of the nation which, it was proclaimed, was a symbol of man's inalienable right to life, liberty, and the pursuit of happiness.

They reached the waiting steamboat, and Radburn hustled them aboard. A servant held a light as the slaves were told to get into the hold of the vessel where barrels and boxes of freight were stored. A bell rang, and the boat began its move down the Potomac River. Clem was overcome with the idea of going South, where he knew there were millions of slaves

Fig. 7. The slaves were ordered to march to the boat. Solomon and Clem, handcuffed together, led the line of slaves.

working the plantations. He hated leaving his home and everybody he had ever known, knowing he would never see any of them again. Eliza never stopped crying. Solomon tried to comfort them. Nobody but Randall and Emily slept that night.

When sunrise came, Birch called the slaves up on the deck and took their handcuffs off. They were told to sit at a table and were given breakfast. A mulatto woman, who was serving the table, was touched by their misery and told them to cheer up and not be so cast down. After breakfast, the slaves were again handcuffed, and Birch ordered them to go to the stern deck where they sat together on boxes. In Birch's presence no one spoke a word. Now and then a curious passenger would walk back to where the slaves sat, look at them for a while, then silently leave.

As the slaves looked out over the water and across to the land, they felt the contrast of the beauty of the world and the horror of their own condition. The sun was shining bright and warm, and the sights and sounds along the riverbank were pleasant. Birds flew overhead. With spring, the fields along the water's edge were green.

There were several stops along the way. Solomon and his fellow slaves were ordered to form a line to leave the ship. Once at the landing, Birch placed them on stage coaches for the next lap of their journey south. At one place Birch and his five slaves occupied a stage coach, and he laughed with the children and even bought them a piece of ginger-bread. He tried to joke with Solomon Northup, who hated him so he would make no reply.

At last they arrived at a big city, Richmond, Virginia. There they were taken to another slave pen, this one owned by a man called Mr. Goodin. It was much like the one they had left except it was much larger. There were two small houses in the yard of the slave pen which were used for slave buyers to physically examine the slaves. The price of each slave was related to his health and general condition, and the price also varied according to the age of the slave and the sex. Men brought the highest prices. Children were cheapest.

Goodin himself, a short fat man as dark as some of his slaves, met Birch at the door of the slave pen and greeted him cordially. The two had been friends for a long time. Chuckling, Birch told Goodin he had brought company and indicated the five slaves waiting beside him. He asked when the ship was leaving for the South, and Goodin replied it would leave the next day.

Goodin took hold of Solomon's arm and turned him partly around, looking him over from head to toe as one might an attractive dog or horse. Goodin felt he was a good judge of the value of slaves. He looked closely at Solomon Northup plainly calculating what price he would bring at the slave market.

"Boy, where did you come from?" he finally asked.

"New York," Solomon answered. He had either forgotten or else chose to ignore Birch's orders demanding that he not mention New York, or traveling in the North, or anything about his past life as a freeman.

Goodin was plainly surprised. "What the heck!" he exclaimed. "What have you been doing up there?"

The small crisis did not escape Birch who later led Solomon into one of the small houses. "You told that man you came from New York," he said angrily.

"I meant no harm, Mr. Birch," Solomon said. "I forgot."

Birch was upset. "If I ever hear of you telling a soul about New York, I'll kill you! You hear? That goes for you saying you were free, too. Don't you forget it again. It might be the last of you."

Birch did not want to be caught by the law selling a free man. He was in a risky business, and Solomon knew he meant what he said. He would kill Solomon if if he let his secret out and put him in any danger of the law.

Goodin's Slave Pen contained about thirty slaves. One of these was a huge yellow man named Robert, whose face reflected his deep depression over his state. Birch handcuffed him and Solomon together, and they instantly established a friendship. Robert's story was much like that of Solomon Northup. Robert told Solomon that he had a wife and two children in Cincinnati, where two men had hired him and brought him south. He did not have his free papers with him and, without these papers at Fredericksburg, he was seized and thrown into jail. When he talked to his captors, he was confined and beaten as Northup had been. Three weeks before he had been brought to Goodin's slave pen.

As was usually the custom among slaves, each slave was issued a rough blanket which was meant to take care of all sleeping arangements. A slave took his blanket to whatever place appeared most comfortable to him, spread it out, and laid down for the night's sleep. Solomon, Robert, Clem, Eliza, and the children slept on their blankets in one of the houses. Four other slaves, all from the same plantation, spread their blankets in the house where Northup lay. The four had been sold and were on their way south.

During the day Solomon spoke with Goodin's slaves. David and Caroline were married and desperately in fear they would be sold to different masters. Both were mulattoes with light complexions, suggesting that each had one or more ancestors who was white. This was not unusual. Mary was a tall jet black girl who was listless and apparently indifferent to all that was going on around her. She had no training. She had never been free and knew only to obey her master. Lethe was the opposite and was consumed with hate and anger. Her husband had been sold, and Lethe did not know where he was. She knew she would never see him again. A smart woman, she felt it didn't matter who bought her since her life would only be worse. The scars she bore on her face were there because she had rebelled and been beaten. Her whole being was filled with hate, and she said, pointing to the scars on her face, she wanted to wipe them off in some man's blood!

While other slaves in the yard were becoming acquainted, Eliza was sitting off in a corner by herself, singing and praying for her children.

One day Goodin superintended the sweeping of the yard and ordered the slaves to wash themselves while he watched. Then he ordered them to roll up their blankets and be ready to travel. At least one slave was happy. Birch had decided to take Clem Ray back to Washington, and Clem was rejoicing at his good fortune. (Years later Clem ran away and escaped to Canada, spending the night with Northup's brother-in-law and his family in Saratoga. He was able to report to Solomon's family where he had encountered Solomon and the condition in which he had seen him.)

With Solomon and Robert at the lead, Birch and Goodin drove the slaves through the streets of Richmond to board the brig, Orleans. This was a very large two-masted sailing ship loaded with tobacco. By five o'clock the slaves were aboard the Orleans, and each of the forty slaves who had been in Goodin's slave pen (except Clem) was handed a cup and a spoon.

Once aboard, with nothing more to do, Solomon took a small knife and cut his name on his cup. Seeing this done, all of the slaves wanted him to write their names on their cups. Slowly, he managed to get the small job done for all of them.

At night the slaves slept below the deck in the hold of the brig, and the hatch was barred down. Each slave took his blanket and slept on boxes of goods stored in the hold or wherever he could find room to spread his blanket.

Birch left Solomon and the other slaves at Richmond, returning to Washington, D. C., with Clem. Northup would see him again years from then under entirely different circumstances for both of them.

The Orleans was headed south.

CHAPTER FIVE

The small sailing vessel, Orleans, headed down James River. Then it passed into Chesapeake Bay. When it arrived at Norfolk, it was anchored for a short time.

Four more slaves were placed on board. Two young men, Fred and Henry, were born slaves. The young woman, Maria, was pleased to be going to New Orleans. With her good figure she felt some man would buy her. She thought herself extremely pretty. The man named Arthur was impressive. He was dragged aboard the sailing ship with his face swollen and bruised. One side was raw and bleeding. Once on the ship, Arthur was forced into the hold by his handlers. A strong, intelligent man, he was a free man who had long lived in Norfolk, where he had a family. As a mason, he worked late one night. When he was going home through a dark alley, he was attacked by a gang of men. He fought back with all his might, but there were too many for him alone to resist. At last he was gagged and bound. Later, his captors had him at a slave pen. Then during the night he was brought to wait for the Orleans. It was plain to see that Arthur was a man who would not be a slave.

After the ship left Norfolk, Solomon was put in charge of the kitchen. Robert was selected waiter by the captain. They were to distribute food and water. The cups were filled with coffee, and bread and meat were handed out. There were no plates.

Slaves were fed twice a day. At ten and at five o'clock the same food in the same amount was given them. The diet was almost always fried pork, a slice of bread, and a glass of water. At night the slaves were driven into the hold and fastened down.

The Orleans was scarcely away from land when a violent storm rocked the boat. Most of those on board were sea sick. There were many vomiting. The foul odor from the vomit made the hold almost impossible to endure. Some of the slaves prayed. Others held each other in fear. Solomon sometimes thought the slaves would have been better off if the storm had taken them.

One day Arthur and Solomon stood talking on the bow of the ship. They decided to revolt. They knew where pistols lay, and they planned to steal them. They would kill the captain and mate. There were only six sailors aboard to defend the ship. The plans made by Arthur and Solomon included help from Robert. All details were carefully planned.

Just as they readied for the attack, Robert became very ill. The deathly disease was smallpox. Before reaching New Orleans Robert died, a kidnapped slave who had been born free. He was buried at sea. His wife and small children in Cincinnati would never know what happened to him.

Solomon was very depressed. One day a kind sailor asked him what was wrong, and Solomon told him his story. The sailor had great sympathy and gave him a pen and paper so he could write a letter home. Solomon wrote to Henry Northup telling him where he was.

When the Orleans anchored at New Orleans, a wonderful thing happened. Two men came up and called in a loud voice for Arthur. When Arthur saw them, he was nearly crazy with joy. They were men from Norfolk who had come to New Orleans to rescue him. His kidnappers, they told him, were in prison. A happy Arthur soon left with the two men.

Northup felt very lonely. No one was there to help him.

Traders came on board the Orleans. One of these was the owner of the New Orleans slave pen. His name was Theophilus Freeman. Freeman stood before them to read the names of slaves sent to him. As each slave present heard his name, he or she stepped forward. He called out the name "Platt." No one answered.

"Captain, where is Platt?" Freeman demanded.

The captain said he knew no one aboard by that name.

"Who shipped that nigger?" he wanted to know, pointing to Solomon.

"Birch," the captain answered.

"Your name is Platt. You fit the description. Why didn't you answer?" he asked Solomon angrily.

"That is not my name. I never heard it before," Solomon told him.

"Well, I'll learn you your name! And you won't forget it either!" he told him.

The slaves filed off the ship and were driven to Freeman's slave pen. There were fifty slaves at Freeman's pen. One by one, they were called up and given food. They were told to leave their blankets in one of the small houses in the pen. At night they took their blankets and found a place to sleep. This could be under a shed, in the loft, or in the open yard.

From that day on Solomon had a new name. He was now called "Platt."

He could hardly believe what had happened to him. Thousands of miles away from home, he hoped God would give him strength to endure what lay ahead. He was now a slave named Platt.

CHAPTER SIX

Theophilus Freeman, keeper of the New Orleans slave pen, woke early. He went into the slave pen. He was there to wake all of the slaves up in a hurry. He walked among them snapping a whip to get their attention. The whip made a sharp crack that was frightening. He kicked sleeping older men and women.

There was to be a big slave sale the next day. All slaves must be ready for the show room. He wanted his people to look bright and alert.

The slaves were told to wash themselves well. Men must shave. Then Freeman issued clothes. A hat, coat, shirt, pants, and shoes were given the men. A calico dress and a handkerchief for their heads were given to the women. All of it was very cheap but clean.

The slaves were sent to a large room to be trained. The men were placed on one side of the room, the women on the other. The tallest were at the head of each line. The shortest were at each end of the two lines. Emily stood at the end of the row of women.

Freeman charged the slaves to be lively and smart. He told them to remember their places in the lines. All day he spent exercising them in the art of looking good to buyers.

After food was handed out at noon, the slaves were ordered to dance, and Platt was told to play a violin.

Next day the customers came to see Freeman's "New Lot." Freeman became the salesman. He pointed out all the good qualities in each slave. He walked among them in a brisk manner. He held the head of one slave, caused others to open their mouths and display their teeth. Some slaves were taken to the house in the yard. There they were stripped for closer inspection. If a slave lost the sale by objecting to this, he or she was beaten.

Several buyers came to inspect Platt, as he was now known. One was a man from New Orleans. Freeman priced Platt at $1500. The man said that was too much. Platt had hoped the man would buy him and take him to New Orleans. He figured it would be easier to escape from the city than from a plantation that might be remote.

David and Caroline were both bought by a Natchez planter. They left happy because they were together. Lethe was sold to a Baton Rouge planter. Her eyes flashed with anger.

The same man bought Randall. Randall was made to jump, run, and show his teeth. All this time Eliza was crying. She begged the man not to buy him or to buy her and Emily also. In that case she would be the most faithful of slaves. The buyer told her he could not afford it. Freeman held his whip high to warn her to stop.

"I won't have such carryin' on around here," he told her. "Unless you stop this minute, I'll take you to the yard and give you one hundred lashes. I'll take care of this foolishness!"

Eliza cringed in fear before him. She tried to stop crying, but she could not. Over and over she cried out how she loved her little boy. She begged the buyer to take her and Emily, also. The man told her he could not do that. The bargain was made. Randall had to go with the buyer. Eliza ran to him and kissed him over and over. She begged him not to forget her. All the time tears were falling like rain.

Freeman cursed her. He told her she was a blubbering wench and ordered her to go to her place. He told her to behave herself and be somebody. He swore he wouldn't stand that stuff any longer. He would give her something "to cry about," he said.

The planter left with his new purchase.

"Don't cry, Mama. I will be a good boy. Don't cry," Randall called to her as he left with his owner.

What became of Randall nobody knows.

That night almost every slave who arrived on the Orleans became ill. The disease was smallpox. Platt, Eliza, Emily, and Harry were taken to Charity Hospital.

Lying there ill, Platt heard the doctor say that he would live if he survived until nine o'clock. The thought of dying a slave among strangers was a bitter one. He thought surely he would die.

He could hear the bell toll every time a person died. This was a signal to an undertaker to come get the body. Burial would be in the potter's field, a public-owned burial place which was used for paupers, including slaves.

Fig. 8.   Eliza begged the owner of the slave auction not to take her children away from her.

But Platt did survive. So did Eliza, Emily, and Harry. Platt's face bore scars from his illness ever afterwards.

One day soon after their return from the hospital, Freeman ordered the slaves to take their places. A buyer was waiting.

The middle-aged man who came to buy slaves was good-looking. He appeared to be a happy person. He asked if Platt and Harry would like to live with him. He also asked Eliza. Platt's age was listed by Freeman as twenty-three although he was actually ten years older than that. Like the ages of horses, slaves were judged on their ages so that owners could calculate how many years of work could be expected from them. The buyer agreed to Freeman's prices. The price was $900 for each of the two men and $700 for Eliza. Eliza was now called by her slave name, Dradey.

Now Dradey nearly went crazy. She could not bear the thought of losing Emily. She broke from the line of women and went to her little child. Emily put her arms around her mother's neck and clung to her. Freeman went to them and caught Dradey's arm with a rough move. Dradey held her child all the closer. Freeman then struck the woman a hard blow to cause her to loosen her hold on the child. She staggered backwards.

Dradey pleaded with the buyer. "Mercy, mercy, Master," she cried. "I will die if Emily is taken from me. Please, Master, buy Emily! Oh, please!"

Freeman tried to interfere. Dradey paid him no attention. She begged the buyer to take them both.

Fig. 9.   Dradey begged William Prince Ford not to buy her and leave Emily.

She told how Randall had been taken from her. "My darling, she is so young," she begged. "I will die!"

The buyer, his face troubled, asked what price Freeman would take for Emily.

"What is her price? Buy her? I won't sell her. She is not for sale," Freeman answered.

The buyer said he was not in need of one so young. Her mother wanted the child so badly, however, he would pay a reasonable price to keep them from being separated.

Freeman was deaf to the man's words. He would not sell her on any account whatever. There were men enough, he vowed, who would pay him $1500 for her. Such a handsome, fancy piece as Emily would be would bring lots of money when she was older. She was a beauty, a doll, he declared. She was not, Theophilus Freeman cried angrily, "A thick-lipped, bullet-headed nigger."

When Dradey heard this, she became frantic. "I will not go without her," she screamed.

All this time Platt and Harry held their blankets, waiting. They were ready to go with the buyer. The buyer looked at Dradey with deep sorrow. It was as though he wished he had not bought her and caused her so much grief. Freeman tore Emily from her mother's arms. The child became hysterical. "Don't leave me, Mama! Don't leave me!" she cried as her little arms stretched out to reach her mother.

Dradey was pulled and pushed by Theophilus Freeman's assistants and forced to follow her new owner. Dradey sobbed until gradually only great moans were heard. The boat that would carry them away to the home of the buyer lay in the river. Solomon, Harry, and Dradey, pulled along by two of Freemen's men, followed behind the buyer as they headed for the boat. As they walked away, they could hear Emily's desperate cries for her mother to come back. It was a heartbreaking situation to witness, and Northup felt ill from watching the mother and child separated.

Fig. 10.   Platt boarded the "Roldoph" with his owner, Ford, and with Eliza and a slave named Harry.

CHAPTER SEVEN

Platt and Harry followed the man who bought them through the streets. Dradey was looking back until she was finally loaded on the boat, still weeping uncontrollably.

The boat they boarded was the Rodolph. Shortly after they arrived, the steamboat was moving briskly up the Mississippi River. There were many slaves aboard. All of them were recent purchases at the New Orleans market. Among the buyers was a planter from Rapides Parish named Kelso. He had bought a large gang of women who were aboard the boat.

The name of the master of Platt, Harry, and Eliza, the slaves learned, was William Ford. He was a Baptist minister as well as a planter and sawmill owner. He told them their new home would be in the "Great Pine Woods." This was in the heart of Louisiana, in Rapides Parish. Ford operated a plantation on Bayou Boeuf which had been inherited by his wife. He also owned a large farm on Hurricane Creek in the pineywoods. This was where they were going. He and a partner had bought a sawmill in these "Great Pine Woods." It was for the sawmill that Ford had gone to New Orleans to purchase slaves.

Reverend Ford was in every sense a good man. Yet he had lived all his life in plantation country, and he did not see anything wrong with slavery. He never questioned the right of one man to own another, seeing slavery in the same way his father had before him.

Fig. 11. The "Roldoph" on which Platt, his owner, and the other slaves rode, was a small steamboat which plied the Mississippi from New Orleans to Natchitoches, stopping at Alexandria on the Red River.

However, he was a kind man and was never guilty of mistreating his slaves.

For two days and three nights Solomon and his fellow passengers were aboard the steamboat.

On board the steamboat Platt had time to think. He thought of nothing but escape although he had no idea how he could manage it. Once he thought of telling Ford his true history. After thinking about it a long time, he decided that was too risky. Years later he wished he had taken that risk.

Red River flowed into the Mississippi River, and the Rodolph left the great river and steamed up the Red to the small Port of Alexandria. There the boat docked. Alexandria was the center of the rich plantation country along the lower Red River.

Ford and his slaves remained overnight in Alexandria. The next morning they climbed aboard the primitive Red River Railroad to continue their travels. They would ride as far as the railroad track extended south of Alexandria. That was sixteen miles away at a settlement called Lamourie. A large shingle mill, a boarding house, and a store were located there. The settlement was along the banks of a small bayou, Bayou Lamourie.

After leaving the train at Lamourie, Ford and his slaves had to walk twelve miles to Ford's Place on the Texas Road. There was no other way to get there but to walk. There were no carriages or buggies awaiting the arrival of the train to drive paying customers to wherever they wanted to go. The walk led through acres and acres of cotton fields.

It was a very hot day. The slaves were still weak from the effects of smallpox, and they moved more slowly than they might have done otherwise. Ford told them to sit down and rest when they wished to do so. They crossed the Carnal and Flint plantations, walking through mud holes which were left by winter rains. Such narrow roads ran through all fields. They were laid out for plowmen who needed to have places to turn their mule-drawn plows into each new furrow. The turning row ended at the banks of Bayou Boeuf.

The path then was across a narrow bridge over the bayou and on through the Great Pine Woods.

This country of the Red River delta was really a strip of rich land about five miles wide which lay on the south side of the river. It was bordered by the Great Pine Woods. Where the low lands of the delta reached the woodslands there were some swamps. Solomon saw small ponds of water covered with green scum. But beyond, there were the low hills covered with tall trees which made up the Great Pine Woods. As they walked, they sometimes scared wild cattle searching for food on the ground below the trees. Solomon noticed that some of the cattle were branded with initials burnt into their hides with red hot branding irons. These letters stood for the names of their owners. Other small wild cattle were not branded.

At noon they reached a clearing in the woods. All the trees had been cut down in a space large enough for a house, a barn and corn crib. Solomon identified other smaller outbuildings as they passed by, including the outdoor privy and a smokehouse.

There was a chicken yard and a barnlot, where mules neighed and kicked at each other.

A pretty creek with water as clear as crystal ran below a hill. The water was pouring into the creek from a spring. Solomon, Harry, and Dradey went quickly to the spring, where they drank thirstily of the icy waters.

Above the creek, atop the hill, was an unpainted dog trot house, the summer home of William C. C. Martin. Behind the house was a narrow log building which served as a kitchen. William "3 C's" Martin, as he was called, was a member of the Rapides Parish Police Jury. He owned 82 slaves and was one of the largest slave owners in the parish. His plantation was called Sugar Bend Plantation. His lands alongside Bayou Boeuf were planted in sugarcane.

Like other planters living on Bayou Boeuf, Martin moved his family to the hill country in summer. People considered it safer to live in the pineywoods during the hot months. Certainly, it was very unhealthy to remain in the low lands along the bayou. Millions of mosquitoes lived in stagnant water holes and ditches along the bayou. In the warm months many people along the bayou died, although they did not associate the illnesses with the swarms of mosquitoes. Many of those who died were children.

The Martin home was like those of other planters whose summer homes lined Spring and Indian Creek and other smaller creeks running through the Great Pine Woods.

The slaves were sent to the kitchen. There they received baked sweet potatoes, cornbread, and bacon. With this they drank more of the cold spring water. In the meantime Martin and Ford sat on the gallery in big rocking chairs and talked. Martin asked Ford about the slave market. He wanted to know if these slaves he had bought were trained to work in the cotton and cane fields. He wanted to know the price of slaves on the New Orleans slave market.

After a long rest, the slaves and their master continued their walk through the Great Pine Woods. For five miles farther they walked without seeing another house. Just at sundown they arrived at Ford's place.

Ford's two-story house was much larger than Martin's. There was a gallery in front of the house. To the rear there were a log kitchen, hen house, corn cribs, and slave cabins. There was a peach orchard. Ford had planted orange and pomegranate trees near his house. Patches of grass covered this clearing of a dozen or more acres in the wilderness.

The Texas Road ran on a ridge to the front of Ford's house. It was higher than all the pineywoods on either side.

A yellow girl named Rose met them on the front gallery. She called Mrs. Ford, who came out of the house to greet her husband. Ford told Platt, Harry, and Dradey to go back to the cabin of Sally, another slave, and rest. They walked to the back of the house where Sally was washing clothes. Her two babies played on the grass near her. They jumped up and toddled toward the newcomers. The babies looked, then turned, and ran to their mother.

Sally took the three new slaves to her cabin. She told them to put their bundles down. She knew they were tired. Just then John, the cook, a coal-black boy of sixteen, saw them. He did not speak but laughed loudly. It was as though the arrival of the slaves was a great joke.

As soon as dark came, Harry and Platt wrapped their blankets around them and went to sleep.

Platt woke early the next morning. He heard the master calling Rose and saw Rose rush to the house to dress the children. Sally milked the cows. John was busy preparing breakfast. Harry went outside, and he and Platt looked at their new quarters.

A black fellow, driving three yokes of oxen, drove into the opening. The oxen were pulling a wagon load of lumber. The driver was Walton, Rose's husband.

Oddly enough, Rose came from Washington, D. C. She had never seen Dradey. However, she had known Elisha Berry. She and Dradey knew the same places and the same people. They became good friends.

Ford was well-to-do. He owned a water-run sawmill four miles away on Indian Creek. Walton had come from the mill. Ford told his new slaves to return with Walton. He handed Platt a bucket of molasses made from sugarcane for Harry and Platt to eat while at the mill.

Dradey was grieving over her children. Ford did his best to console her, but that was not possible. Ford told her she could stay with Rose. Her work would be at the house.

Walton drove the wagon. He, Harry, and Platt enjoyed talking on the long ride to the sawmill. Walton told them he was born a slave on Ford's place. He spoke of him fondly, like a child speaking of his father, Solomon thought.

When they finally reached Indian Creek, Platt and Harry found more slaves. These were Sam and Anthony. Sam had come from Washington in the same gang as Rose. He knew Birch, the brutal slave trader at Williams' Slave Pen. Anthony was a blacksmith.

When Ford arrived at the mills, all workers — called "hands" in this country — went to work. Some piled lumber. Others chopped logs.

On Sundays all the slaves went to Ford's place. There he read the Bible to them. He sat in the doorway of his house as he spoke. The slaves looked into his face as he read. He spoke to them of God and loving one another.

Sam had become very religious. Mrs. Ford gave him a Bible, and he took it to work with him. When he had free time, he read it. It was hard for him to read so Platt often read to him. Some of the white men who came to the sawmill did not approve of slaves reading. They said Ford should know better than to allow such a thing.

Platt could tell the men did not approve of their reading. He longed to tell them that Master Ford did not lose anything by his kindnesses. His slaves worked hard for him.

Fig. 12.   Platt had learned how to build a log raft while working on the Great Lakes in New York. Now he made a raft to float on Bayou Lamourie.

Because he wanted to help Ford, Platt had an idea. The lumber they were cutting at the sawmill had to be sent to Lamourie some miles away. It had always been the custom to haul the logs overland. Platt thought he had a better idea. He thought the logs could be sent cheaper by water.

Indian Creek emptied into Bayou Boeuf. The Boeuf then mingled its waters with those of Bayou Lamourie. In other words, there was a water route that could be followed. Platt thought the lumber could be rafted over these waters to Lamourie.

Adam Taydem was foreman at the sawmill. He did not approve the idea and declared that he did not think it could possibly work. Ford, however, wanted to try the raft to see if it would work in transporting the logs to Lamourie.

Platt understood rafting logs because he had experience with rafting logs on the New York canal. With Ford's permission he went to work. For days he worked very hard. He removed tree trunks from the streams wherever they might block passage of the raft. Then he went to work on making the raft. It was a sort of platform made with logs that would float on the water. On each was a crude shelter for a man managing a raft. The raft and its load were called a crib. Platt divided the load into a dozen cribs.

The arrival of the raft at Lamourie caused a lot of excitement. All praise went to Platt. It made him feel very good. After that, he rafted all of the lumber to Lamourie.

It was on these trips that Platt was able to learn more about the Indians who lived in these same woods where Ford's sawmill was located. They lived along the banks of a beautiful creek that was called Indian Creek because of the presence of these Indians. They lived in simple houses made of pine poles covered with bark. An interesting people, some of the men could be seen riding their horses past the sawmill. Their dogs followed close behind. Platt noticed that they often had wild turkeys, deer, and other game on their horses. These they expected to trade some planter for corn and whiskey.

Platt came to know Cascalla, the chief of the tribe. He also met his son-in-law, Baltese. Platt and Sam got into the habit of visiting with them after the day's work was done at the sawmill. Platt learned how different their lives were from those of any people he had known.

Platt went to an Indian dance one night. A roving band of Indians had made a camp in the Indian village. Cascalla and Baltese with many helpers roasted a deer over a big fire for the visitors. A fiddler among them played a tune. The music sounded very strange to Platt. The Indians danced, whooping loudly as they did so.

In a hole cut in a fallen tree, the Indian squaws pounded corn with a pestle. Then they made a cake from the cornmeal.

In the fall Ford changed Platt's work from the sawmill to work around the clearing where Ford's house stood. Mrs. Ford needed him to build a loom. She needed it so Sally could weave winter clothes for the slaves. Ford did not know where to get a loom and decided to build one. Platt assured him he could make one. When the loom was completed, Sally thought it was perfect. After that, Platt was put to work making more looms. These were taken to the plantation on Bayou Boeuf.

At one time a carpenter came to Ford's house to do some work. The man's name was John M. Tibaut. Platt was told to quit making looms and help the carpenter. For two weeks Platt worked with him, planing and matching boards for the ceiling in a new room being added to the house.

John Tibaut was very different from Ford. He was a small man. He had no place he called home. Instead, he went from job to job wherever he could find a few days or weeks' work. An ignorant man, Platt found Tibaut was also spiteful, mean, and very disagreeable in his dealings. Platt did not like working with him and was glad when the job was done.

CHAPTER EIGHT

William Ford signed a note for his brother, Reverend Franklin Ford. The note was the one signed when Franklin Ford borrowed money for his private girls' boarding school at Minden, Louisiana. The lender required a second person to sign the contract to repay the money — with interest, of course. This was in case Franklin Ford did not have the money to repay the loan. So William Ford, since he had signed the note, had to pay back the money his brother had borrowed because Franklin did not have the money.

Neither did William Ford have the necessary money available. To get the needed money he was forced to sell eighteen slaves. He sold seventeen to Peter Compton, a planter on Red River.

William Ford owed money to the carpenter, Tibaut. Tibaut had worked at Ford's house and had built some outbuildings on his plantation on Bayou Boeuf. Tibaut said that he would take Platt for the money owed him. The value of Platt was $400 more than the amount Ford owed the carpenter, so Ford took a mortgage on Platt for this balance. This meant that Tibaut owed Reverend Ford four hundred dollars before he completely owned the slave, Platt. This also meant that Reverend Ford still had some money invested in the slave.

Tibaut took Platt to Ford's plantation on Bayou Boeuf. Platt saw Dradey at the plantation. She was so filled with grief over her children she could not work well. Mrs. Ford had not been pleased with her house work. She was sent instead to work on the Bayou Boeuf plantation. By this time Dradey had become very thin and ill.

Ford's overseer on his plantation was a man named Chafin. He was a good man.

Platt with Tibaut as his owner now had to work very hard indeed. Tibaut was never satisfied no matter what Platt did or how hard he worked. He never spoke a kind word to his slave. Every night Platt went to the cabin with the mean voice of Tibaut ringing in his ears.

One night Tibaut ordered Platt to rise early and secure some nails from Chafin. The next day Platt was to begin nailing boards on a weaving house. When Tibaut left, Platt wrapped up in his blanket and went to sleep. With him in the cabin were Dradey, Lawson and his wife, and another slave named Bristol.

Rising earlier than usual the next morning, Platt went to get the nails. Chafin rolled out a barrel of nails. He told Platt to tell Tibaut if he wanted another size nails, he would exchange them. He instructed Platt in the meantime to start with the nails he was giving him.

Platt went to work as directed. Later Tibaut came to where Platt was nailing boards on the small building. He seemed to be in an even worse mood than usual. "I thought I told you to put weatherboarding on that house!" he began.

"Yes, Master, that is what I am doing."

"Where?" he demanded.

"On the other side," Platt said.

Tibaut walked to the other side of the building. He muttered complaints. "Didn't I tell you to get a keg of nails from Chafin?" he asked angrily.

"I did. The overseer said he would get another size for you if these were not what you wanted," Platt told him.

Tibaut walked to the keg. He looked for a moment. Then he kicked the keg violently. He turned furiously on Platt. "I thought you knowed something."

"I tried to do what you told me, Master. I didn't mean anything wrong. The overseer said —" Tibaut interrupted with curses. He ran towards the house and took down one of Ford's whips. The whip had a short wooden stock braided over with leather. The lash was three feet long, ending in long leather strings that could bite into the flesh.

At first Platt was frightened. Only Rachel, the cook, and Mrs. Chafin were near where Platt was working, but they were not in sight. The overseer and the rest of the slaves were out in the fields. Platt knew Tibaut intended to whip him. He felt he had done nothing wrong. He made up his mind he would die before allowing Tibaut to whip him.

Tibaut walked up close to him with the whip in his hand. He ordered Platt to undress.

"Master Tibaut," Platt said to him, "I will not."

Tibaut rushed at him, seizing him by the throat. With one hand he held the whip ready to strike. Platt caught him by the coat collar and drew him close. Then he seized Tibaut by the ankle, pushing him back with the other hand. Tibaut fell on the ground. Platt put one arm around his leg and held it to his breast. He placed his foot on Tibaut's neck. Tibaut was completely in Platt's power.

Mrs. Chafin and Rachel heard the noise. They were alarmed. For a slave to hit a white man in Louisiana meant certain death.

Tibaut's screams had been heard in the fields. Chafin came rushing up on his horse as fast as he could. By then Tibaut had risen to his feet. He brushed dirt from his hair. He was pale with rage looking at Platt. Not a word was said.

"What is the matter?" Chafin asked.

"Master Tibaut was going to whip me for the nails you gave me," Platt told him.

"What is the matter with the nails?" Chafin wanted to know.

Tibaut answered that they were too large.

"I am overseer here," Chafin told him. "I told Platt to take those nails and use them. I told him if they weren't the right size, I'd get others when I came in from the field. It is not his fault. I'll furnish what nails I please, Tibaut."

Tibaut did not answer. He shook his fist at Platt. He said this was not half over. Tibaut walked away followed by Chafin.

After awhile, Tibaut came out of the house. He saddled his horse and left.

Chafin came out and told Platt not to stir. He told him not to run. He said Tibaut was a rascal and had left for no good. There might be trouble before night, Chafin told Platt.

Platt stood there, his anger gone. Now he realized he had put himself in a position to be killed. He prayed. He knew no Negro could strike a white man and survive. He wept at his situation. When he looked up, Tibaut and two other overseers were there.

"Cross your hands," Tibaut commanded him.

The two overseers both held whips. One held a coiled rope also.

One of the men said he would cut Platt's throat, tear him limb from limb.

Platt knew he could not resist the three men. He crossed his hands, and Tibaut tied his wrists together. Then Tibaut bound his ankles together. The other men had slipped a cord within his elbows, ran it across his back, and then tied it firmly. It was impossible then for Platt to move hand or foot. Tibaut then formed an awkward noose with the rope and put it around Platt's neck.

"Now then," one of Tibaut's men asked, "where shall we hang the nigger?"

Chafin was watching from the gallery of his house. He did not come to Platt's rescue. Rachel was crying by the kitchen door. Platt felt his time had come. Tears fell down his cheeks. His tormentors mocked him.

Chafin left the gallery. When he reappeared, he held a pistol in each hand. He came walking toward the tree where the three men were getting ready to hang Platt. "Gentlemen," he said to them in a voice that shook with rage, "I have a few words to say. You had better listen. Whoever moves that slave another foot from where he stands is a dead man. It is a shame to murder him in this manner. In the first place, he does not deserve it. I never had a more faithful boy than Platt. You, Tibaut, are at fault yourself. You are pretty much a scoundrel, and I know it. You richly deserved a flogging. In the next place, I have been overseer here seven years. In the absence of William Ford, I am master here. My duty is to protect his interests. That duty I shall perform. You are not responsible. You are a worthless fellow. To begin with, Ford holds a mortgage on Platt for $400. If you hang him, he loses his debt. Until you pay off that mortgage, you have no right to take his life. You have no right to take it anyway. There is a law for the slave as well as for the white man. You are no better than a murderer!

"As for you," Chafin said to Tibaut's companions, "be gone! If you have any regard for your safety, I say, be gone!"

Cook and Ramsay mounted their horses and rode away. In a few minutes Tibaut also left.

Platt remained standing. The rope was still around his neck. Chafin called Rachel. He told her to go to the field and get Lawson. Tell him, he said, to hurry to the house. Tell him to bring the brown mule with him. The brown mule was known for his speed.

Soon Lawson appeared.

"Lawson, you must go to the Great Pine Woods. Tell your Master Ford to come here at once — that he must not delay a moment. Tell him they are trying to murder Platt. Get there by noon if you kill the mule getting there!"

Chafin stepped into the house. He came out with "a pass." (A pass was a sheet of paper on which was written permission for the slave to leave the plantation.) Lawson took it quickly. He knew he might be stopped by a white person — any white person he might meet. He would be asked for the pass. Without it, he could be placed in jail.

Fig. 13. William Prince Ford cut the rope that held Platt dangling from the tree.

CHAPTER NINE

By midday on almost any summer day, the sun in Louisiana is so hot even field work is suspended for a two-hour dinner break to avoid the worst of the heat. There is risk of heat stroke and subsequent death from the intense heat. The bare feet on the scorched earth can blister. The only days which are cooler are those when there is rain. This day while Platt stood tied so he could not move was one of the hottest days of the summer.

Platt stood as Tibaut had left him. His head was bare. He had on scant clothing that could not soften the sun's scalding rays. The rope still dangled from his neck. It was now soaked with sweat. Small stiff threads from the rope rubbed against Platt's flesh. His wrists and feet were tied. He could not move. The sweat that poured from his head fell down his face with great drops landing on his eyelids and lingering there. He was blinded. His eyes stung. His wrists and ankles swelled. The pain increased as the rope dug deeper into his swollen flesh.

Chafin paced back and forth on the gallery. He was in sight of Platt. Not once did he approach Platt. It was clear that Chafin was very uneasy, expecting trouble of the worst kind. He watched the road constantly. He remained on the gallery, not returning to the field after the noon bell rang calling the men back to work. It was an unheard-of break for the overseer not to return to the fields. Why he did not elect to relieve Platt was hard to understand. It was not for want of sympathy. That was clear. He may have felt that Ford needed to see exactly what Tibaut and the other two men had done. It may have been a legal matter. After all, Platt was the property of Tibaut.

Why Tibaut did not return was not clear either. Lawson on the brown mule rushing past Tibaut and the two men may have given them the idea that Lawson had gone for help. They may have thought Chafin had sent for planters on the Boeuf to come to his aid.

Whatever the reasons, Platt remained in agony under the scorching sun. He had nothing to eat or drink. Once Rachel, acting fearful she might be told to mind her own business, brought Platt a cup of water. She held it to his lips so he could drink the last drop. "Oh, Platt, how I do pity you!" she whispered.

Just at sunset Ford came riding into the yard. His horse was covered with foam from the race over the Texas Road to the plantation. Chafin met him at the door. He and Ford talked briefly. Then Ford went to Platt.

"Poor Platt," he said, "you are in a sad state."

"Thank God! Thank God! Thank God, Master Ford, you are here," Platt cried.

Ford took a knife from his pocket. He angrily slashed the cord that tied Platt's arms. He slipped the noose from his neck. He cut the cord around his ankles.

Platt tried to walk but fell.

Ford returned to the house. Platt was alone again. Tibaut and his friends drove up and went into the house. Platt could not hear what was being said.

He could hear the voice of Tibaut as it rose loud and angry. Then he could hear the quieter voice of Ford's.

After awhile Platt crawled into his cabin and lay down, hoping to sleep. But he was in such intense pain he could not rest. When the slaves came in from the fields, they came to his cabin. They knew about his frightening experience from Rachel's trip to the fields to get Lawson. Dradey and Mary brought Platt a piece of bacon, but he could not eat. They scorched cornmeal and made "coffee" for him to drink. This helped some. By then the cabin was filled with slaves. Rachel came. It was her pleasure to describe how Platt had fought Tibaut. She dwelt on the final kick, even showing them how it was done. The crowd laughed. It was not a laugh because Rachel's story was funny but because they were glad. They were glad Tibaut's got what they felt was more than his due. Rachel then told how Chafin came out with two pistols to rescue Platt. Her audience liked that part, too. And then she told how Ford, filled with anger, had cut the ropes with his knife.

By this time Lawson came to the cabin. He had to tell, with sound effects, how he had gone like a "streak of lightnin'" to Ford's house in the pineywoods. Lawson recounted how Ford became furious as he gave him the message that Tibaut and the other two overseers were trying to hang Platt.

Among themselves in the freedom of the cabin the slaves expressed their own feelings. It was as though the beating of Tibaut by Platt was their own personal victory. They kept talking, repeating the stories of the day's event. Platt, lying there in pain, half listened to the hum of their voices, but their support somehow soothed him.

Chafin suddenly appeared at the cabin door. "Platt, bring your blanket and come with me. You will sleep in the Big House tonight."

As Platt walked alongside Chafin, Chafin told him, "I will not be surprised if Tibaut comes back before morning."

Once during the night a dog barked. Chafin rose quickly out of bed to look out the window. He could see nothing. "I believe that scoundrel is around, Platt. If that dog barks again and I fall asleep, call me."

When the dog barked again, Chafin was quickly out of bed again. He did not need to be called. Again there was nothing to be seen.

Sore and weary, Platt went back to work the next morning. Chafin, as an overseer generally did, usually mounted his horse and left for the fields. Instead, he first went to the weaving house where Platt had returned to the work he had started there the day before.

In a little while Tibaut rode into the yard on his horse. He walked over to the weaving house and looked sharply at Platt. He did not say a word. Most of the day he sat on the gallery. Ford finally left to return to the Great Pine Woods. Platt, seeing him leave, felt uneasy.

One more time Tibaut came to give orders. Then he returned to sit on the gallery.

Never afterwards did Tibaut refer to the conflict.

During the week the weaving house was completed. Tibaut informed Platt he had hired him to Peter Tanner. He would work under a carpenter named Myers. Platt was relieved.

Peter Tanner was a brother of Mrs. Ford's. He lived across the bayou on a large plantation.

Thus it was that Platt went to Tanner's. Tanner had heard of the flogging. The event, in fact, distinguished Platt along the bayou. There was a saying going around among the Bouef planters concerning Platt. "A devil of a nigger," they were saying with more than a little admiration that he had challenged Tibaut. Tibaut was considered a low classed man on the Boeuf, a man who did not know how to conduct himself as he should. Platt felt that the reputation he had gained was both a burden and a compliment.

Peter Tanner was a jovial man who laughed a lot. He wanted to impress Platt with just how severe he could be, however, if a slave should challenge him. "You're the nigger that flogged your master, eh? You're the nigger that kicks. You are the guy that holds Carpenter Tibaut by the leg. You are the one who walloped him, are ye? Well, I'd like to see you hold me by the leg, I should. You're an 'portant character. You're a great nigger, ain't ye? I'd lash you. I'd take the tantrums out of ye. Jest take holt of my leg, if you please. None of your pranks around here, my boy. Remember that. Now go to work, ye kickin' rascal!"

Platt worked under Myers for a month. Both were happy with the experience.

Fig. 14.   Reverend William Prince Ford and Peter Tanner both read the Bible to their slaves every Sunday.

On Sundays, Peter Tanner, like Reverend Ford, called his slaves together to read the Bible to them. Only Peter Tanner had a different purpose. It was not God and love he wanted to read about. It was to prove by the Bible that there were supposed to be masters and slaves. He began by reading the twelfth chapter of Luke. When he came to the 47th verse, he looked around him. He continued, "'And that servant which knew his Lord's will,'" he paused and looked around to be sure the slaves were getting the point he wanted to make. "'That servant which knew his Lord's will...'" Again he looked into the faces of the slaves. "'Which knew his Lord's will and prepared not himself,'" he said. "'Prepared not himself, neither did according to his will, shall be beaten with many stripes,'" he read with emphasis.

"That nigger that don't take care — 'that don't obey his lord' — that's his master, don't you see? — 'he shall be beaten with many stripes.' Now, many signifies a great many — forty, a hundred, a hundred and fifty lashes. That's Scripter!" Peter Tanner went into detail describing just what he thought the Bible meant on this point.

When he was through, he cried out, "Here, Platt, you held Tibaut by the leg. Now see if you can hold these rascals in the same way till I get back from meetin'."

He called Warner, Will, and Major to come forward. These were melon-stealing, Sabbath-breaking niggers, Tanner explained. He did not approve of such wickedness. It was his duty, he felt, to put them into stocks.

Fig. 15.   Platt let the boys out of stocks as soon as Peter Tanner was well out of sight on his way to church.

Platt looked at the stocks. Tanner directed the three boys to seat themselves in front of the stocks. He watched as they put their arms and legs through the holes. Then he clamped the lock which held the two upright planks together. Tanner secured them himself and felt sure they could not get out until he let them out. With a satisfied chuckle he took another good look at them and climbed into his waiting carriage.

He handed Platt the key to the stocks. Then he, his family, and Myers headed up the dusty road toward Cheneyville. They were riding in the horse-drawn carriage the five miles to Beulah Baptist Church. They would not return until late afternoon.

No sooner was the carriage out of sight than the boys spoke. "Platt, you ain't leaving us in here, now is you?

Platt hated seeing them sitting on the hot ground unable to move. He remembered his ordeal in the sun. He made the boys promise they would return to the stocks as soon as he ordered them to do so. Then he let them go.

Warner, Will, and Major wanted to repay Platt's kindness. So they took him to the watermelon patch. They all helped themselves. Platt enjoyed the cool, sweet melons as much as they had.

Shortly before Peter Tanner returned, Platt placed the boys back in the stocks. They looked as though they had been sitting there all day as Tanner had ordered. When Tanner drove up, he laughed gleefully.

"Aha! Ye haven't been strolling about today, anyway. I'll teach you what's what. I'll tire ye of eating watermelons on the Lord's Day, ye Sabbath-breakin' niggers!"

CHAPTER TEN

The work was completed at Peter Tanner's. Platt was returned to Tibaut to work at Ford's plantation. The two were alone together most of the time. Chafin cautioned Platt to beware of the man. At any moment he might harm him. Platt from then on had to keep one eye on his work and one on Tibaut.

The third morning after returning to Ford's, Tibaut left for the day. The job the two were working on was building a cotton press. When Tibaut returned to work, he was in one of his foul moods.

Early that afternoon Platt was using the jack plane on one of the sweeps. Tibaut was standing by the workbench. He was fitting a handle into a chisel.

"You are not planing that down enough," he said to Platt.

"It's just even with the line," Platt told him.

"You're a d—n liar," Tibaut exclaimed.

"Oh, well, Master," Platt replied agreeably. "I will plane it down more if you say so." He proceeded to plane the board down more.

Not a shaving was removed before Tibaut yelled out sharply. "You've planed it too deep now! You've spoiled the sweep entirely!" He cursed loud and long. Finally, Tibaut seized a hatchet and came toward Platt. "I will cut your head open!" he screamed.

The bright, sharp blade of the hatchet caught in the sunshine. In another instant it would be buried in Platt's brain. If he stood still, he would certainly die. If he ran, Tibaut would hit him in the back with the hatchet. In that moment Platt sprang at the carpenter, catching his uplifted arm. With the other he seized Tibaut's throat. The two men were glaring into each other's eyes. Platt kicked Tibaut, took his hand away from his throat, and snatched the hatchet. He then threw it beyond reach.

Mad beyond control, Tibaut seized a large stick that was lying on the ground. Again he came towards Platt. Again Platt met him. This time he grasped Tibaut by the waist. Being the stronger of the two, Platt threw Tibaut to the ground. He then took the stick away from Tibaut and threw it away also.

Tibaut ran to the workbench. He was trying to reach the broadaxe. A heavy plank was in his way. Seeing this, Platt sprung upon his back. Pressing him downward, the slave tried to force Tibaut to release the axe handle.

Unable to loosen Tibaut's hand, Platt seized him by the throat. This time he held him until, choking, he released the axe. His face was black from suffocation instead of anger. Tibaut's eyes were round with horror.

Throwing the man off the workbench, Platt left Tibaut on the ground. Then he ran swiftly and jumped over a fence and fled. Once he looked back. He could see Tibaut saddling his horse. Quickly Platt glanced back again; this time to see him gallop away.

Platt passed a field. Slaves shouted at him. They knew something had happened. They made signs for him to run; run fast.

Platt had known what would happen. He soon could see Tibaut with two men, all on horseback, led by a pack of yelping dogs. They were following his tracks. There were eight or ten hungry dogs. They were a kind of bloodhound trained to track down slaves. They were used to hunting runaways. No Negroes escaped the dogs on Bayou Boeuf. This was one of the proud boasts of Boeuf planters who vied with each other over whose dogs were best. One reason the dogs caught all runaways was that slaves were not allowed to learn to swim. Therefore, they could not escape into water and cause the baying dogs to lose their scent. Dogs lost the scent of the pursued when they came to water. Platt was counting on this fact to save him.

Platt ran toward the swamp at the back of the fields. He could hear the yelps of the dogs behind him. They were gaining on him. He could hear them coming closer and closer behind him. Every howl sounded nearer and nearer. Platt ran faster and faster, faster than he would have ever believed he could run. His eyes searched out the nearest approach to the swamp ahead of him. He spotted a lot of palmetto growing in shallow water. He stepped into the water, and it came over his shoe tops. The farther he ran in the water, the deeper the water became. He was grateful because this way the dogs could not follow him. He sank to his waist in the water. Then suddenly the water was shallow again. The dogs were no more than a half mile behind him. He could hear them coming, rushing through the palmetto.

The dogs reached the water and became confused. Their savage yelps grew fainter. Then a long howl signaled they were coming closer once again. To Platt's joy he came to a bayou. He plunged into the bayou and swam to the other side. At last he felt safe from the dogs.

After crossing the bayou, Platt found the water so deep in the swamp that it was impossible to run. He was in Cocodrie Swamp. Here was a virgin forest of sycamore, cypress, gum, cottonwood, and many other trees which enclosed him. Underneath was a deep muck, a mixture of water and mud which clung to his feet and legs. For thirty or forty minutes he slowly moved along. There were no houses to be seen. Wild beasts — bears, wildcats, oppossums, fox, rabbits, deer and other animals — lived in these woods. There were hundreds and hundreds of snakes hanging from the tree limbs overhead and around the bases of the trees. Platt identified moccasins that he knew were poisonous. Every log and bog was alive with snakes. Platt saw them move away as he neared. Sometimes he almost put his hand, or his foot, on one of them. He lost a shoe when the sole came off in the muddy water.

Alligators, great and small, lay in the water or on logs. Platt learned his approach startled them. The creatures moved off, plunging into deepest water. Sometimes his keen gaze had missed seeing them. Then he would run a short way around and avoid them. He learned alligators cannot turn rapidly.

About two o'clock that afternoon he heard the last of the hounds. They did not cross the bayou. For the rest of his flight, this worry was over. There were other worries though with the alligators and snakes. Before stepping into a muddy pool, he struck the water with a stick. If the water or ground moved, he knew he had to go around it.

The sun finally went down. The great swamp was then spooky in the blackness with the outlines of the dark trees against patches of gray sky. Platt feared the sting of the moccasin or the jaws of the alligator with every step he made. After what seemed a long time the moon rose. Its pale light filtered down through the low hanging Spanish moss. Platt kept traveling until midnight, trying carefully to make use of what moonlight came through the dark trees. His hopes were that he would come upon a less scary spot somewhere where he could rest. But the water grew deeper. The walking became even more difficult. At last he felt he must move cautiously now. He could not risk meeting a white person who might arrest him.

He stopped. The scene was dreary beyond description, but he at least would see no white person and risk being caught. The swamp was filled with the sounds of the quacking of countless ducks! No human footstep may have penetrated the recesses of this awesome swamp before. When the sun was shining, the swamp was so quiet the silence was chilling. Yet at night Platt's appearance aroused all the feathered tribes who lived in the swamp. They were there by the thousands. From their throats poured thousands of different sounds which were eerie to

Platt, tired and scared as he was. There was the tremendous sound of fluttering wings. Then there were sudden plunges some made into water. These startled Platt. It seemed to him that all the fowls of the air had descended on Cocodrie Swamp that night. And all the creeping things of the earth seemed to have gathered there as well.

The moon rose far above the tree tops. Platt by now had time to think. He knew he must get to William Ford's house in the Great Pine Woods. Up until this time he had been traveling south. Now he decided he must travel in a northwest direction to get to Ford's place.

Platt's clothes were in tatters. His face, hands, and body were covered with scratches. His bare feet were full of thorns. Muck and mud covered him. The green slime from the surface of the stagnant water stuck to him. He was completely miserable. But there was nothing to do but keep trying to move on.

He reached Cocodrie Bayou again. This was the same bayou he had swam across to escape the dogs, but he was miles downstream now. He heard a rooster crow. It was a joyful sound. Now he knew he was nearing a clearing. There was nothing to do but move on, mindful of the danger.

The bogs were behind him. There was dry land, and the hills were not too far away. He knew he was at the edge of the Great Pine Woods.

Just at daybreak he came to an opening. Farther on, a slave and his young master were catching wild hogs. Platt knew any white man he met could demand a pass. He did not feel he could run any more.

So he quickly decided to try something else. He would do his best to appear fierce, dangerous. He walked boldly toward the man, glaring angrily in his direction. His method worked. The man appeared frightened. Platt asked in a rough manner, "Where does Reverend William Ford live?"

"He lives seven miles from here," the man said quickly.

"Which is the way to his place?" Platt demanded. He was even more fierce than before.

"Do you see those pine trees yonder?" he asked. The trees were a mile or so away.

"I see them," Platt answered.

"At the feet of those pine trees," the stranger told Platt, "runs the Texas road. Turn to the left. It will lead you to Ford's."

Platt rushed on. He was glad to get away from the man. The man was just as glad. Later Platt saw logs burning. He did not stop. He was too afraid of meeting another white man. Pushing on, Platt was at Ford's at eight o'clock.

Platt knocked at the door. Mrs. Ford opened it. She did not recognize him. He was in such a sad state he didn't look the same. Ford appeared beside his wife. He saw who it was.

Platt told him the story of his second crisis with Tibaut. He told him about his flight. Ford listened. He spoke kindly to Platt. Then he took him to the kitchen for food. Platt had not eaten since daylight the day before.

The slave, John, brought food. Mrs. Ford set a glass of milk and cookies down on the table for him. The food was good, but the kind voices were even better.

Platt went to a cabin and slept for many hours.

Fig. 16.   Platt ran toward the swamp at the back of the fields.

CHAPTER ELEVEN

When Platt woke, he was sore and stiff. But he was among friends. John cooked him dinner. Sally came to talk.

Platt spent some time walking in the yard. The flowers were in spring glory. There were blossoms of every color. The fruit trees were in bloom. Peach trees shook out pink flowers. The plum trees were at their prettiest in white. Orange and pomegranates added to the sight. The fragrance was sweet and soothing.

Platt wanted to repay the Fords. He began trimming vines. He weeded the flowers. Mrs. Ford came out to say it was good of Platt to do the work. But, she said, he was not able. She told him he should go to his cabin and rest. He told her he did not feel well, but he thought it good to exercise. She told him that Ford was planning to go to the Boeuf in a few days.

On the fourth day Ford told Platt to be ready to go with him to the bayou. There was only one horse. Platt said that he could walk.

Ford rode slowly so that Platt could keep up with him. He urged the slave to take his place sometimes in order to rest. Platt said no, he was not tired. The minister tried to cheer the slave up. He told him the goodness of God was seen in his escape. He said Platt was like Daniel who came unharmed from the lion's den. He asked if Platt had felt the need to pray.

Within five miles of the plantation a horseman came galloping towards them. It was Tibaut. Tibaut did not speak to Platt. He did not curse in Ford's presence. "I never saw such running before," he told Ford. "I'll bet him against $100. He'll beat any nigger in Louisiana. I offered Cheney $25 to catch him, dead or alive. He outran the dogs in a fair race. Them Cheney dogs ain't much, after all. Dunwoodie's hounds would have had him down before he touched the palmettoes. Somehow the dogs got off the track. We had to give up the hunt. We rode the horses as far as we could. We kept on foot till the water was three foot deep. The boys said he was drowned, for sure. I wanted a shot at him bad. Ever since I have been riding up and down the bayou. I hadn't much hope catching him. I thought he was dead. Oh, he's a cuss to run, that nigger is!"

Tibaut went on and on. When he had finished, Ford spoke. He told him he was sorry that there had been more trouble. He told him that Platt had been inhumanly treated. He told Tibaut he was at fault. Using hatchets and axes on slaves was shameful, Ford said. "This is no way of dealing with slaves. This will set all of them to running away. The swamps will be full of them. A little kindness would have better results."

"Mr. Tibaut," he said, "you and Platt cannot live together. You dislike him and would not hesitate to kill him. Knowing this, he will run from you again through fear of his life. You must sell him or hire him out. If you do not, I will take steps to get him away from you."

Platt did not open his mouth.

When they arrived at Ford's plantation, Platt went to Dradey's cabin. Again, all the slaves gathered. They took it for granted Platt would be whipped. That was the penalty for running away—five hundred lashes!

"Poor fellow," Dradey said. "It would have been better if you had drowned. You have a cruel master. He will kill you."

They tried to figure who would give Platt the whipping. Platt wanted a chance to get to feeling better and wished heartily they would hush. Yet he would not say anything. He knew that they were only talking over this accepted fact of slave life.

Early the next morning, Tibaut left Ford's plantation. Later a tall, good-looking man came to Platt. "Are you Tibaut's boy?" he asked.

Platt took off his hat and answered that he was.

"How would you like to work for me?" he asked.

"Oh, I would like to. Very much."

"You worked under Myers at Peter Tanner's, didn't you?"

Platt said that he had.

"Well, Boy, I have hired you from your master to work for me in the Big Canebrake. It is thirty-eight miles from here — down on Red River."

The man was Mr. Eldred. He lived on the next plantation from Ford. It was likely his hiring Platt was Ford's idea.

Next morning Platt went with his new master. They were joined by his slave, Sam. Platt and Sam rode on a wagonload of provisions drawn by four mules. Eldred and Myers on horseback followed the wagon.

Sam told Platt he was born in Charleston, South Carolina. He thought that Tibaut was a really mean man. He wished his master, Randal Eldred, would buy Platt. Platt told him he wished so, too.

They moved slowly along the bayou road. They crossed Keary's plantation and went on to Bayou Huffpower. Then they came to Bayou Rouge swamp. About sunset they turned from the highway and headed toward the Big Canebrake. It was hard to find a path through which the wagon could pass. The path was so narrow that the wagon could hardly go through. Tall canes were as thick as they could stand.

After hours of riding, they came to "Sutton's Field." Sutton had been a fugitive from the law. That had been many years before. He had lived alone. Later Indians had killed him. His ghost, it was said, still walked his fields. This story of being "haunted" by Sutton's ghost lay heavily over the clearing.

Finally, the party reached the wild lands of Eldred. Eldred planned to clear the place to establish a plantation. The men went to work next morning with cane knives. The plan was to build two cabins. One was to provide for Myers and Eldred. The other was for Sam and Platt. Wide-spreading branches of the ancient trees almost shut out the light of the sun. Here and there was a palmetto. Around it was the thicket of tall canes.

From the oak trees hung yards of grey moss. Bay, sycamore, and cypress had grown here untouched for centuries.

The men cut down oaks and split them into rails. With these they made temporary cabins. They covered the roof with broad palmetto leaves. These were good substitutes for shingles.

Insects, thousands and thousands of them, caused the biggest problem. Flies, gnats, and mosquitoes swarmed around them. They got into the ears of the working men — into their eyes, noses, and mouths. It was impossible to brush or beat them off. It seemed they would eat the workers in wee, small bites.

No place could be lonelier than the Big Canebrake. The men endured it by the hardest. Compared to working for Tibaut, however, it seemed like paradise to Platt. He worked hard and became very, very tired. Yet he could lie down at night and sleep in peace. He could wake up in the morning without fear.

Within a few weeks four black girls came down from Eldred's plantation. They were Charlotte, Fanny, Cresia, and Nelly. They were all large and stout. Axes were handed to them. The women were then sent out to work with Sam and Platt at cutting down trees. The men were surprised at how well the women did their work. Their heavy, well-directed strokes felled the largest trees. Platt and Sam knew that women worked alongside men on the plantations. There they ploughed, drove mule or ox teams, cleared wild lands, worked on roads, and all the rest. Still Platt was amazed at how they did the heavy work in the

Big Canebrake. They piled logs as well as any man. Platt had been puzzled as to why some planters preferred women workers. Until now he thought slaveowners must be very foolish to have women trying to do heavy work most people thought was men's work. Now he saw there were women who could manage very well working alongside men at all the heavy work.

Eldred had told Platt that he might visit at Ford's place after working four weeks at Big Cane. This time, armed with a pass, Platt was to leave on Sunday for a short visit at Ford's. He was to return to Big Canebrake on Tuesday.

Without warning Tibaut appeared in their midst in the Big Cane Brake. He asked Eldred how Platt and Myers got along working together. "Very well," Eldred told him. He added that Platt was going to visit Ford on Sunday. Tibaut quickly vetoed the idea.

Eldred insisted that Platt had earned the day or two off, that he had worked extremely hard. He should be allowed to go, Eldred repeated.

Platt saw them go into a cabin. He went into the one he and Sam shared.

Next morning Platt appeared at the door where Tibaut had spent the night with Eldred. He had his blanket rolled. It hung on a stick over his shoulder. He stood waiting for his pass. Tibaut came out, scowling. He went over to a tree stump and sat there. He was figuring what he was going to do. Platt stood there for a long time, waiting as patiently as he could.

Suddenly he shifted the stick over his shoulder and turned to leave.

"Are you going without a pass?" Tibaut called out angrily.

"Yes, Master, I thought I would."

"How do you think you'll get there?"

"Don't know," Platt replied.

"You'd be taken and sent to jail. That's where you ought to be. They'll take you before you get halfway there," he said. He went into the cabin. When he reappeared, he held a pass in his hand. "D—n nigger deserves one hundred lashes," he hissed. Then he threw the pass on the ground.

Platt picked the pass up. Then he left quickly. To get to Ford's it would take hours of walking, and he had to be on his way.

Platt looked at the pass Tibaut had handed him. It read:

> "Platt has permission to go to Ford's plantation
> on Bayou Boeuf and return by Tuesday morning.
>   John M. Tibaut"

This was the usual form. Platt made sure it was deep in his pocket where he would not lose it.

Along the way a great many people stopped him and demanded to see the pass. Those with the airs of planters took no notice of him at all. But a shabby fellow or loafer always stopped slaves. Catching runaways was, for some, a money-making business. If no owner appeared after advertising, the slave could be sold to the highest bidder. Certain fees were allowed finders. "A mean man" — a name given loafers — considered it a godsend to find a Negro without a pass. Platt showed the pass, watching warily to see it was returned to him.

Platt had no money or food with him. Yet no slave with a pass need go hungry. He could present his pass to the master or overseer on any plantation. The slave stated his needs. He was sent to the kitchen and provided with food and shelter. The traveler could stop at any house and ask for a meal as freely as at a hotel. It was the custom of the country. Whatever their faults, people in the bayou country welcomed travelers.

When Platt arrived at Ford's, he went to Dradey's cabin. Lawson and Rachel came quickly to see him. Platt was shocked at the sight of Dradey. She who had once been plump was now so thin. The first time he had seen her in Washington, D. C., she had worn pretty clothes and jewels. She had been a graceful figure. Now she was wrinkled and without spirit. Grief for her children had eaten out her heart. She seemed a hundred years old.

Next day Platt rolled his blanket back up and left Ford's. When he reached Bayou Huffpower, there was Tibaut astride his horse standing in the middle of the road. He asked why Platt was returning so soon. Platt told him he did not want to miss his deadline for returning to the Big Canebrake. Tibaut told him that he should go no farther than the next plantation. That very day he had sold him to Edwin Epps, a planter on Bayou Huffpower.

Platt did as he was told. He found Edwin Epps, a big, heavy man living in a small house not far from the bayou. Epps examined his new slave and asked

Platt many questions. After awhile, he told Platt to go to the Slave Quarters (a line of cabins).

The first task Edwin Epps ordered his new slave to undertake was to make an axe handle. The handles used in the Boeuf country were simply straight round sticks. Platt set to work to make the kind he had been used to seeing in New York. These were crooked. Handles were made like this because they were more convenient. When Platt was finished, Epps looked at the handle with surprise. He was much interested in its difference to the ordinary kind he knew. For a long time he kept the handle at his house. When his friends came, he showed it to them.

Edwin Epps was a cotton planter. Platt had seen plenty of cotton during his two years on Bayou Boeuf. Now he knew he had lots to learn about the planting, cultivating, and harvesting of cotton.

Platt soon learned the rhythm of life on a cotton plantation. Everything revolved around the cotton crop. After the winter rains, the last of the old crop was plowed under. Platt learned to plow a straight furrow. He learned to plant the cotton atop the rows.

The seeds were planted so that a straight line of small plants was produced, growing too close together to survive. Therefore, to allow about twelve inches between the plants, excess plants were "chopped out" with a sharp hoe at the same time grass and weeds were removed. Platt learned this was the art of "thinning" the cotton. The cotton was hoed four times. With all of the workers in the spring sunshine, each taking a row of cotton to chop and then moving on to other rows, the work could be the most pleasant of the year's chores. When Epps left them alone to chop the cotton, they could talk among themselves with freedom. Of course, all that ended when Edwin Epps was around.

It was late July before the cotton had grown beyond the stage where the grass had to be chopped from it. These few weeks between the end of cultivating the crop and cotton picking were called "lay-by" time. Even though the cotton crop was not needing them during "lay-by" time, Edwin Epps had many chores waiting for them to do.

The weather was so hot that the ground itself sent forth its own heat. The foliage of the trees was thick, and even the spots of shade they provided were not cool. There were no cooling breezes. Whether Big Houses or cabins, the houses were so hot from the rays of the summer sun that few people tried to sleep until the earth had cooled off around midnight. There were other compensations, however. The peaches, plums, and figs were ripe. Watermelons, cantaloupes, and vegetables were plentiful. There were many foods both in the fields and woods. This provided even the slaves with something to vary their dreary provisions of bacon and cornbread.

The first sign cotton picking time was near came with the first cotton bloom. Edwin Epps was as pleased as could be when he found the first blossom on a day in early August. After the blossoms fell, the cotton bolls came and in time spilled out their white cotton. Platt thought the white cotton fields looked like the snow he had seen every winter in New York.

Fig. 17. There were some times that were fun — like in summer when watermelons were ripe in the fields and it was possible to sneak to swim in the bayou.

Each slave was issued a cotton sack made of heavy cloth. It was held by a strap which was worn around the picker's neck. The sack to be filled then fell down the front of the picker. Platt found out soon he was not good at the art of picking cotton. No matter how hard he tried, he could not get the knack of it.

Fig. 18. Planters did not want their slaves to learn to swim, but, like other children, slave children learned to slip off for a swim in the bayou.

CHAPTER TWELVE

Platt was sent to work in the corn field. Later he scraped cotton, a form of chopping and thinning the crop. It was while he was working in the cotton field that he began to feel ill. He had chills and fevers and lost a great deal of weight. Sometimes he was so dizzy he reeled and staggered like a drunken man. Despite his illness he was expected to keep pace with his fellow workers. Every day he found this was getting harder and harder to do.

Epps swung his whip and lashed his back. The sting of the whip roused Platt enough to try to keep working. In time the sharpest whack of the rawhide did nothing but cause Platt to become sicker still. Finally by September when cotton picking was getting underway Platt was unable to leave his cabin. Up until this time he had received no medicine or attention from his master or mistress. The old cook visited his cabin sometimes and brought "coffee" made from parched corn or sometimes a piece of broiled bacon.

When it was said that Platt was going to die, Epps told him to go to Holmesville several miles downstream and see the doctor. Platt walked down the bayou road to where Dr. Windes had his office. The doctor examined him. He told him to eat only enough food to sustain life and to eat no meat. Later he told Epps that the illness was the effect of the climate.

Fig. 19.   Cotton picking required a skill Platt simply did not have.

Platt went back to the cabin and did as the doctor had told him, eating very little. Slowly he began to feel better. Before he was completely well, Epps appeared at the cabin door with a cotton sack. He ordered him to get back to work.

Platt had never picked cotton in his life. No matter how hard he tried his big hands somehow did not get the cotton from the bolls with any skill whatever. Epps did not want to accept this fact. Epps threatened and cursed. Although he usually popped his whip against a slave's back when the slave did not bring enough cotton to be weighed at the end of the day, he excused Platt at first because he was "a raw hand." Epps swore Platt was a disgrace and not fit to associate with a cotton-picking "nigger." Finally he concluded that the new slave could not pick enough cotton to pay for the trouble of weighing it. He then sent Platt to the woods with an axe, a wagon and a mule team, to cut and haul wood for winter use.

During the first two years Platt was Epps' slave, Epps had a habit of going to Holmesville and returning drunk. This happened at least every ten days. Shooting matches were held at the small village, a landing on Bayou Boeuf. Men gathered from far and near to compete with pistols and guns and display their marksmanship. Often these were turkey-shoots with marksmen taking turns at hitting the wild turkeys. These affairs ended with drinking parties.

When Edwin Epps returned from Holmesville drunk, it was time for his slaves to hide, if they could. He was half-crazy and wild. At such times he would break the dishes, chairs, and furniture in his house.

Fig. 20.   When Epps got drunk, he wanted to dance and ordered the slaves to dance while Platt played the fiddle.

Then he would seize his whip and walk into the yard. Any slave he could find felt the smart of the lash. Sometimes he would keep them running in all directions to dodge this drunken man.

There were other times when he came home less brutal but more dangerous in some respects. On these occasions he was ready for merry-making. Platt must bring his fiddle to the Big House, and all the slaves must assemble. These were the times when he held a big dance. Suddenly he became elastic, gaily "tripping the light fantastic toe," dancing around the gallery and all through the house.

Mrs. Epps persuaded her husband to bring home a fiddle from New Orleans on one of his visits there. This he provided Platt to play whenever he or Mrs. Epps wished.

No matter how tired or worn out the slaves were, the dance went on. "Dance you d—n niggers, dance!" Epps would shout.

Usually his whip was at hand ready to strike any slave who dared to rest a moment. This included pausing to catch one's breath. When he himself became exhausted, there would be a break, but it was brief. With a slash, and crack, and flourish of the whip, he would shout again, "Dance, nigger, dance!" Platt was ordered to play quick-stepping tunes.

Often Mrs. Epps came to lash out at her husband from the door. She threatened to leave and return to her father's house. Sometimes she herself could not keep from laughing at his antics. Many times these sessions lasted until near morning. Needing rest, the slaves were made instead to dance and laugh.

Despite obeying the whims of this unreasonable master, the slaves had to be in the field as soon as light appeared. Nor was the day over until the last rays of the sun were gone. The tasks had to be performed as usual even if the workers had stayed up all the night before dancing at his orders. His demands for work were the same. The whippings were just as severe. Indeed, after such frantic revels, his mood was always uglier even than usual.

Ten years Platt worked for this man. There were no rewards. Ten years his labor went to make profit for Edwin Epps. For ten years he was compelled to address him with downcast eyes as his master. Like other slaves, Platt had to uncover his head as a sign of respect. This was the attitude and language of the slave toward the master.

Edwin Epps was a man who did not know kindness or justice. His was a kind of rough energy with which he conducted his planting operations. His mind was untrained. Known as a "nigger-breaker," he was proud of breaking the spirit of slaves until they did not dare protest his actions. He regarded a black man purely as property. He thought of them as being no different from his horse or dog. Such a man was Edwin Epps.

There was one man on Bayou Boeuf even worse than Epps. He was Jim Burns. Burns used only women on his plantation. He kept their backs so raw and sore they could not work as well as ordinary slaves. He was a brute. A fool, he whipped and took away the strength upon which his farming depended.

Epps remained on Bayou Huffpower for two years. During these two years he accumulated enough money to buy a plantation of over three hundred acres. He took possession in January, 1845. To his plantation he took eight slaves. These were the people with whom Platt lived and worked for ten years. They were Abram, Wiley, Phebe, Bob, Henry, Edward, and Patsey.

For years these slaves had been together. They shared memories of South Carolina. They had belonged to a planter named Buford. Financial troubles had come to Buford, and this meant trouble for his slaves. He was forced to sell them. In a chain gang they had been driven to the plantation of Archy B. Williams, who owned a huge plantation less than twenty miles from Epps' place. Edwin Epps had been an overseer for Williams. When Epps left to operate his own plantation, he took these slaves in payment for his work.

Uncle Abram at sixty years in 1845 was the oldest of the eight. Once he had been known for his great strength. He stood a head taller than most men. Born in Tennessee, he had gone with his young master to war under General Andrew Jackson. Andrew Jackson was his hero. Never did he tire of talking about the General. In fact, he talked about General Jackson so much it was a joke among the other slaves.

Yet Uncle Abram was like a father to the Epps slaves. He spoke in serious tones to them, always kindly, for he was a kind man. He tried very hard to keep the other slaves from trouble. In 1845, on Epps'

Fig. 21. *"Edward, now thirteen, was born to them on Epps' place."*

place, he was an old man. He forgot his hat, his hoe, his basket.

Wiley was forty-eight years old. He was born on the plantation of William Tassle in South Carolina. His job had been to operate a ferry. Wiley was a very quiet man. He talked little. He did say that he wished he were back in Carolina.

Phebe had been a slave of Tassle's neighbor, Buford. When Phebe married Wiley, Buford had bought her husband. Called "Aunt Phebe" at Epps' place, Phebe, as Platt knew her, was a sly old creature. She had been a good field hand, but now she worked as a cook. She was a big talker.

Bob, 23, and Henry, 20, were Phebe's children by an earlier marriage. She had kicked her first husband out the cabin door. Just why Platt never heard. Then she had married Wiley. Edward, now thirteen, was born to them on Epps' place. Edward was assigned to work at the Big House as a companion for the little Eppses.

Patsey was twenty-three. She also had belonged to Buford. She had no connection with the other slaves, however. She was proud of being "a Guinea nigger." She had been brought to Cuba in a slave ship with her mother. They were both traded to Buford.

Patsey stood out among the slaves as an unusual person. She was slim and straight. She wore an air about her nothing could destroy—not even slavery. She was a fine athlete. She could leap the highest fences. Nobody could outrun her. She was a skillful teamster. She unharnessed, fed, and curried her

Fig. 22.   Patsey was by far the best cotton picker in the country.

mules at the crib. She plowed a straight furrow. Nobody could beat her splitting rails. She was by far the best cotton picker in the country. She was, indeed, queen of the field.

By nature Patsey was a joyous creature. She was a laughing, light-hearted girl. Yet she cried often and suffered more than any of the other slaves. Her back bore the marks of thousands of stripes.

Patsey's problem was Edwin Epps. Epps found Patsey uncommonly attractive. When he was drunk, he often went to her cabin. If she dared oppose him with the slightest word, he would lash her. Because of Epps' unwanted attention to Patsey, Epps' wife hated Patsey with a passion. If Patsey did not watch carefully while walking in the yard, she could be hit with a piece of stove wood or a broken bottle. These were thrown at her by Mrs. Epps.

In the Big House Patsey was the subject of many heated quarrels between Epps and his wife. There were times when the husband and wife did not speak for weeks. Patsey was almost always the cause. Yet she was the innocent victim. There was nothing she could do about it.

Fig. 23. The planters drove 147 slaves from Bayou Boeuf to St. Mary Parish.

CHAPTER THIRTEEN

There was no cotton crop at all on Bayou Boeuf in 1845. This was the first year Edwin Epps was on the Boeuf plantation. There were no cotton crops in all the Bayou Boeuf country. Thousands and thousands of caterpillars — wooly worms — ate entire crops. Slaves were idle that fall. There was not enough to keep them all busy.

A rumor came to Bayou Boeuf that labor was in great demand on the sugarcane plantations on the Louisiana coast. Wages were said to be high. There was a particular need in St. Mary's Parish.

Even though the upkeep of slaves was minimum, the cost of maintaining a labor force for a year when there was no crop was a costly business. Planters on Bayou Boeuf were anxiously trying to find a solution to the problem. When the rumor came that slaves were needed on the sugarcane plantations, the planters jumped at the idea of hiring out their slaves to cut sugarcane on the plantations on the coast.

The planters decided to drive a drove of slaves to St. Mary's. There they would hire them out to planters. In September, therefore, 147 slaves were assembled by their masters at Holmesville. Abram, Bob, and Platt were among them. About half of the slaves were women.

Epps, Alanson Pearce of Lone Pine Plantation, Henry Toler, and Addison Robert were in charge. They had a two-horse carriage and two saddle horses for their use. A large wagon was drawn by four horses. This was loaded with supplies and provisions for the slaves. The blankets upon which the slaves would sleep were rolled up and packed on the wagon.

Before leaving, the slaves were issued food. At two o'clock the procession began the long journey, led by the carriage with planters. Behind them the slaves walked in lines. Two horsemen brought up the rear.

That night the group reached McGrow's plantation. It was a distance of ten or fifteen miles. The slaves were ordered to halt. Large fires were built. The slaves made pallets on the ground where they slept. The white men stayed at the Big House. An hour before daybreak the drivers came among the slaves popping their whips to wake them. The slaves rose and rolled up their blankets for Platt to place them in the wagon. The procession set forth again.

On the second night there was a rainstorm. Everyone was drenched. Clothes were saturated with mud and water. Finally the group came to an open shed under which they took such shelter as it provided. With so many slaves there was not room for everyone to lie down. Most were fortunate to find themselves a small space in which to sit. Others were forced to stand. There all of the 147 slaves remained through the rainy night, huddled together. At daybreak the next morning, under a downcast sky, the march continued as usual.

Slaves were fed twice a day. That meant boiling bacon and baking corn-cake at the outdoor fires.

The procession passed through Lafayetteville, Mountsville, and New-Town to Centreville. Bob and

Fig. 24. Platt was very good at cutting sugarcane.

Uncle Abram were hired to cut cane at Centreville. As the group moved on southward, its size decreased as others were hired by planters. At nearly every sugarcane plantation at least one slave was hired.

They passed Grand Coteau, a place that was of more than ordinary interest to Platt. Only now and then there was a tree. Those that existed on the prairie there had been brought from somewhere else and planted near the scattered houses. Grand Coteau looked deserted. Once it had been thickly populated. Once the land had been cultivated. Then it had all been abandoned. Herds of cattle fed in the pasture in the center of the place.

When the group reached Bayou Sale a few miles from the Gulf of Mexico, Platt was hired by Judge Turner. His large plantation lay on Bayou Sale, which flows into a bay. At first Platt was employed at repairing Turner's sugar houses. Later with a cane knife he was sent with thirty or forty others to cut sugarcane. He had no trouble at all cutting sugarcane. The art of cane cutting seemed to come naturally. In a short while Platt was able to keep up with the sharpest knife.

This was no small achievement and one regarded with highest admiration by slaves and masters alike. Cane-cutting was a highly competitive task, and the worker who could cut cane the fastest became "the lead man," the cane cutter who set the pace for all the rest of the gang. For a new slave to be able to keep up with the lead man or "the sharpest knife" was quite a feat.

Fig. 25.   Slave children were used to place the stalks of cane upon a carrier that conveyed the stalks into the mill.

Before the cutting was over, Judge Turner transferred Platt. He was given the job of driver at the sugar mill. This was not a job he wanted. A whip was handed to him to use on anybody seen idle. If he did not obey the order to the letter, there was a whip for his back.

The sugar mill with its grinding and boiling never stopped after the season began. Only at the end of the season, which lasted several months, did the mill shut down. Shifts of men worked at various parts of the day and night. It was part of Platt's job to call off one gang and call on another gang to take their place. Platt was not assigned any definite time to rest. He had to snatch what sleep he could from time to time.

Slaves in Louisiana were allowed to work on Sundays and after work hours during the week days and keep the pay for such work. A slave on Bayou Boeuf was given neither knife and fork nor utensils. Gourds, if they could be found, were used for storage. Platt stored his cornmeal in a gourd. The cabins were furnished with no furniture. A blanket was the provision for a bed. Sunday money took care of any of these things a slave owned. A knife, tobacco, or hair ribbons could be bought with Sunday money. Because this was the only money he was likely to see, Platt welcomed the chance to earn money at Christmas. This was done by playing his fiddle.

Platt stayed at Judge Turner's plantation until January 1. His earnings there came to ten dollars. There was a grand party for whites at Yarney's near the Turner place. Platt was employed to play for

Fig. 26. Cane cutting required cutting the top of the sugarcane stalk and stripping off the flags, the long leaves that enclosed it. The cane stalks were planted by laying them lengthwise along a long row and covering them with dirt.

them. The merry makers were so pleased that they took up a collection for him. That amounted to seventeen dollars. Platt felt positively rich.

With this much money his fellow slaves looked upon Platt as a millionaire. It gave Platt himself great pleasure to look at it. He counted it over and over again, day after day. He dreamed of buying furniture for his cabin. He thought of owning a water bucket, pocket knife, new shoes, coats, and hats. It was wonderful to be the richest "nigger" on Bayou Boeuf.

Boats ran up Bayou Teche to Centreville. Platt heard that a captain on one boat was from the North. Platt was bold enough to ask him to let him hide among his freight and ride to New Orleans. Platt did not tell him his history, but he told him how much he wanted to escape. The boat captain felt sorry for Platt, but he told him such an escape would be impossible. Custom officials at New Orleans would take both Platt and the captain's boat. That killed that small hope Platt had entertained.

After this, the slaves who had come from the Boeuf country were assembled at Centreville. Several of the planters arrived to collect payment for their work. Now the slaves were to be driven back to Bayou Boeuf.

Walking in the procession with the other slaves, Platt saw Tibaut. When the slaves were passing through a little village, Platt looked at a small dirty store on their path, and there he was. Whiskey and his lifestyle had taken their toll.

When Platt got back to the Boeuf, he found life was going on much the same. "Old Hogjaw" — the name the slaves called Epps behind his back — had been on a rampage. He had been getting drunk more often than usual. Patsey had found him at her door every time he got drunk. When he was sober, he beat her. This was done to please his wife, who hated Patsey with all her heart.

To be rid of Patsey became a passion with Mrs. Epps. This was strange indeed since Mary Epps herself had made a pet of Patsey when Patsey came to the plantation as a little girl. Mrs. Epps would call her to the Big House and give her milk and biscuits. Such a bright-eyed, sprightly person was Patsey with her happy disposition that Mrs. Epps had found her a pleasure then. But because of her husband's visits to Patsey's cabin, Mary Epps had turned against her.

Mary Epps was not an evil woman. It was just that she was insane with jealousy. Yet there was another side to Mary Epps. Her father, Joseph, lived in Cheneyville. He was a school teacher. In every respect he was a man of honor and influence. He had seen to it that his daughter was well educated. Mary Epps was a beautiful woman as well. She was talented and usually good-humored. She was kind to all of the slaves except Patsey. When her husband was gone, she sent dainties to the slaves. In another society, she would have been known as a fascinating woman.

As for Edwin Epps, he loved his wife as much as he was capable of loving anybody. He was willing to gratify her every whim provided it didn't cost him too much. His was a coarse nature. It was an ill wind that blew Mary Epps into his arms.

What Mary Epps refused to see was that Patsey was the equal to any two slaves Epps owned. He could never replace her. She was an extraordinary worker. That did not keep Mrs. Epps' blood from boiling at the very thought of Patsey.

Sometimes she directed her wrath at her husband who, after all, was the one responsible for the situation. Then there would be a storm of angry words overheard from the Big House. The stormy period was always followed by a calm. During these calms Patsey trembled with fear. She cried as if her heart would break. For she knew the only way that Edwin Epps could quiet his wife was by giving her a promise he would flog Patsey. Thus did Patsey suffer.

The steady diet of bacon and corn cake fed slaves at Epps' plantation was very tiresome. While away in St. Mary's Parish, Platt had more time to think about the problem. He decided that when he came back to Epps plantation, he was going to find another way to get food. It was true the woods were filled with coons and 'possums. Both made delicious food for the slaves. Some slaves had no other source of food than to kill their own game, collect wild fruits and berries in the woods and fields, and catch fish in Bayou Boeuf. Slaves were not allowed to use guns for hunting. Their hunting had to be done with clubs and dogs.

The biggest problem with obtaining food by hunting and fishing was that there was too little time. After a hard day's work on the plantation the slave had to cook his supper. After that he fell asleep.

Fig. 27. As soon as Platt returned to the Bayou Boeuf, he made himself a fish trap.

Platt decided to make himself a fish trap. In his mind he had worked out all of the details. Once back at Epps' place he set to work to make that trap. When the trap was completed, he set it in Bayou Boeuf. After that, he could hardly wait for fish to get into his trap and so prove that the trap actually worked. The fish did come, and he did catch them to eat. Afterwards neither he nor his friends wanted for fish. They were there waiting in Platt's trap sunk beneath the Boeuf waters not far from his cabin.

About the time Platt, Uncle Abram, and Bob returned home, a shocking event happened across the bayou from Epps plantation. From Epps' slave quarters could be seen the Marshall plantation. This family was considered one of the country's aristocratic families.

A man from Natchez had been discussing with Marshall the purchase of his place. Marshall and the man had been talking for several days. Suddenly one day a man came in great haste to Epps' plantation. He said a bloody and fearful fight was going on at Marshall's. If the men were not separated, the slave said, one of the men would be killed. Blood had already been spilled.

Platt would never forget the horrible scene he came upon at Marshall's. On the floor of one room lay the corpse of the Natchez visitor. Marshall himself was covered with blood and still enraged. He was stalking back and forth like a mad man. A dispute had arisen between the two men regarding the property. Both drew their pistols. Marshall's shot killed the Natchez man.

Fig. 28. Both men drew their pistols. Marshall's shot killed the Natchez man.

Marshall never went to jail. Edwin Epps was one of his loudest defenders. He went with Marshall to Marksville to a sort of trial. Nothing came of it. Marshall was declared free of all charges. Strangely enough, he seemed to gain greater respect among fellow planters for having taken such action!

Not long after, Marshall and a kinsman feuded over a card game. Returning home after this dispute, Marshall went to the man's house and challenged him to come out to settle the dispute. Marshall was armed with a pistol and a Bowie knife. Marshall called to him that if he did not come out, he would be branded a coward. If he did not come out, he, Marshall, would shoot him like a dog at the first chance. The man's wife restrained him from going out to meet Marshall. In time the two made their peace with each other.

Knives and pistols were common among the Boeuf planters. If a dispute arose, the men were likely to pull out their weapons. Every one of them carried a Bowie knife. Certainly one influence was the fact that the Boeuf plantations were on the edge of the frontier. Life is always rough on a frontier. Another cause was slavery, for fear of uprisings of these people they held captive was as much a part of life as the air they breathed. With fear went violence.

CHAPTER FOURTEEN

Platt was not a good cotton picker, but he was unbeatable when it came to cutting sugarcane. During the fall harvest of sugarcane Edwin Epps found it profitable to hire Platt out to other planters. Epps received a dollar a day for Platt's work.

For three years Platt was hired to work at Hawkins' plantation near Cheneyville. This was the largest sugarcane plantation on the upper reaches of Bayou Boeuf. Hawkins' sugar mill was one of the largest in the country. For Platt to hold the lead row at sugarcane cutting at Hawkins' plantation was a distinction. This meant he set the pace for a gang of fifty to a hundred cane cutters.

The work which took place on a sugarcane plantation was entirely different from the operations on a cotton plantation. People who lived and worked on sugarcane plantations participated in a very different life from those whose lives centered around cotton.

Platt liked working at Hawkins' big sugar mill. Hawkins was known for the fine white sugar produced at his mill. Most mills produced only an inferior raw brown sugar. Much of the molasses was left in the damp raw sugar.

The mill was housed in an immense brick building. Steam that ran the mill was produced in a boiler outside the main structure. The fragrance of the juice from the boiling sugarcane filled the building and sweetened the air around the mill with its

Fig. 29.   The slave children loved the slave festivals which were held at Christmastime.

fragrance. That alone made Platt's work here more pleasant.

There were larger sugar mills than Hawkins' in other sections of the state. A man named Lambeth of New Orleans was the partner of Hawkins. Lambeth owned an interest in over forty different sugar mills in Louisiana. Most of these were located farther toward the Louisiana coast than this one.

Sugarcane harvest and the Christmas holidays came along together during the winter. Christmas was one time during the year when the slaves had a holiday. On some plantations the holiday lasted a week or even more. Some planters gave four days, five or six days off to do whatever the slaves pleased. Epps allowed three days. This holiday was the only time in the year to which they looked forward with excitement. The rest of the year they were glad when night came. The nights meant some chance to rest. It meant also they were one day nearer to Christmas and the holidays. Christmas was hailed with delight by young and old.

During the holiday Uncle Abram even forgot General Jackson, about whose adventures he never seemed to tire of talking. Patsey forgot her sorrows. This was the time for feasting and frolicking. It was the carnival season for slaves. These were the only days when they enjoyed a taste of freedom. And how they loved it!

It was the custom of a number of planters to give "a Christmas supper." Slaves from neighboring plantations were invited. One year the supper was given by Epps. The next year Marshall provided it.

Then it was Hawkins' turn and so on from one plantation to another. Usually from three to five hundred slaves turned out for these occasions. They arrived on foot or in carts. Some rode horses. Others rode mules. Sometimes they were riding double on the animals — or even triple. Uncle Abram rode a mule with Aunt Phebe and Patsey behind him. This was no uncommon sight on Bayou Boeuf.

Every slave was wearing his or her best attire. The cotton coat had been washed. The stump of a tallow candle had shined the shoes. If a slave owned a hat, it rode jauntily on his head. The women wore kerchiefs around their heads. Bits of ribbon or cast-off bonnets were displayed. Red — deep, blood red — was the favorite color of the women.

Platt never ceased to be amazed at the food that was prepared for these occasions. A table was usually spread in the open air. Loaded with all kinds of meats and vegetables, it was most inviting. There was neither bacon nor cornbread. There were cakes and pies, cookies and candies, of every kind. The cooking was sometimes done in the plantation kitchen. Some of it was often done outside.

Platt liked working with other men at the outdoor cooking. They dug a deep, broad hole in the ground and laid wood to be burned in the bottom of the hole. After the wood burned down, only the red hot coals were left. This meant it was time to start cooking the meat. Chickens, ducks, turkeys, and pigs were laid on a screen over the hot coals. Sometime a whole wild ox was roasted. The meat and fowl had been rubbed well with butter and seasonings. The melting butter and juices made sizzling sounds as they hit the red hot coals. He and the others watched carefully, turning the fowl and meat over from time to time. They kept changing the positions until all of the food was roasted a golden brown and glistened with juices.

Only a slave who had lived a year on endless meals of bacon and corn cakes could properly appreciate such a feast.

The host planter, his family, and numbers of invited guests from the planter community attended these slave feasts.

While the cooking was going on, other work took place. Platt helped lay heavy planks over barrels to form long tables. Benches were made in much the same way. Men sat on one side of the table, women on the other. Lovers managed to find places on opposite sides of the table from one another. The children were so excited they could hardly stop playing long enough to eat. There was much laughing and talking.

Following the feast was the big Christmas dance. Platt played his fiddle. He was considered the Ole Bull of Bayou Boeuf because of his fiddling. One slave played a banjo. Other slaves played homemade instruments.

From a number of planters Epps received letters every Christmas season asking him to allow Platt to play the fiddle for feasts on their plantations. Often these were requests for the planters' own balls. Sometimes Platt returned from his nights of playing his fiddle with a little money jingling in his pockets.

Fig. 30. *When children saw Platt on the road carrying his fiddle, they knew
something special was going on. They always asked him to play for them,
and he obliged.*

Through his music he became well known along the Boeuf. For Platt these occasions gave him a break from the otherwise unending work routine.

Platt was often stopped by passers-by when he was seen passing on the road with his fiddle. So familiar was Platt with his fiddle that those who saw him knew some kind of celebration was going on. "What is coming off tonight, Platt?" they would ask. "Where are you going?" Sometimes, if he had the time, Platt would stop to play a tune for children who gathered around him.

One Christmas when the dance was held at Epps' place, Platt enjoyed an unusual drama. So did everybody there.

Miss Lively and Mr. Sam — two slaves — started the big dance. Miss Lively belonged to Stewart, Mr. Sam to Robert. It was well known that Sam cherished a real liking for Miss Lively. So did Pete from Marshall's place and Harry Keary's. Miss Lively was just that popular.

Platt felt Miss Lively really had the right name. She was certainly lively. She was a big flirt besides. It was a victory for Sam when she gave him her hand for the first dance. His rivals looked crestfallen and angry. If Sam knew this, he did not show it. His legs flew like drumsticks down the outside and up the middle of the dance floor. By his side was his bewitching partner. Excited by this, they kept "tearing down" after all the other dancers were exhausted. Finally Miss Lively pulled at Sam to pause for breath. But Sam was too excited to stop. Leaving Lively alone, Sam whirled like a top. Pete Marshall seized his chance with Miss Lively on the floor. He dashed in with all his might and main. Such a show he put on! He leaped and shuffled and threw himself into every shape imaginable. He meant to show Lively that Sam Robert was no match for him.

Pete had not used good judgment. Such violent exercise took his breath away. He had to stop. He came to the sidelines and dropped down like an empty bag. Now it was time for Harry Keary to show what he could do, and he began dancing with Lively. Lively soon out-winded him. There were hurrahs and shouts. Altogether, Lively sustained her reputation as the most popular slave girl on the bayou.

The dancing continued until daylight. It did not stop when the fiddler quit playing. The slaves provided music peculiar to themselves. They sang funny little songs with lots of rhymes which were not meant to make sense.

The most popular dance was called "patting." It was done while singing one of those special songs. The words were sung rapidly, and the patting was done in rhythm. The patting was performed by striking the hands on the knees. Then the hands were struck together. Next the right shoulder was struck with one hand, the left with the other. All the time the slaves kept time with their feet. They sang in chorus:

"Harper's Creek and roarin' ribber,
That, my dear, we'll live forebber,
Den we'll go to the Injun nation,
All I want in dis creation

Is pretty little wife and big plantation.
Refrain: Up dat oak and down dat ribber,
Two overseers and one little nigger.''

"Old Hog-Eye" was a startling song. Platt
decided you had to be in the South to understand it.

"Who's been here since I been gone?
Pretty little girl with a hosey on,
Hog Eye!
Old Hog Eye!
And Hosey too!
Never see de lak since I was born,
Here comes a little gal wid a hosey on!
Hog Eye!
Old Hog Eye!
And Hosey too!''

Words, nor songs, were not always meant to
have meaning. Without sense but full of catchy
melody was the one Platt learned:

"Ebo Dick and Jordan's Jo,
Them the niggers stole my yo'.
Hop Jim along,
Walk Jim along, Talk Jim along, etc.
Old black Dan, as black as tar,
He damn glad he was not thar.
Hop Jim along, etc.!''

During the rest of the holiday the slaves had
passes. Within a limited distance they could go where

they pleased. If they stayed and worked on the plantation any time during the holiday, they were paid for it. Rarely did they choose to work, even for pay. They were different people for their brief moment of freedom. There was no fear. There was no lash. The slaves even looked different. Such were three days of the year on Epps' place.

Marriages between slaves often were contracted during the holidays. If what passed for marriage ceremonies on plantations were marriages, this is what took place. The only ceremony required was the consent of the respective owners.

Marriages were usually encouraged by owners of women. Since children became the property of the owner of the child's mother, the arrival of children was always profitable for the owner of the woman.

Either party in a slave marriage could have as many husbands or wives as the owner permitted. Either party could discard the other whenever he or she wished to do so. Divorce, bigamy, and related laws did not apply to slaves. If they did not live on the same plantation as their spouses, the husband could visit his wife on Saturday nights. This was true if the wife did not live too far away. Uncle Abram's wife lived seven miles from Epps' place. He could visit her every ten days. As time went on, the couple did not see each other any more. Uncle Abram was growing old, and he felt the effort more than he could make. In time, he almost forgot she existed.

CHAPTER FIFTEEN

Large plantations required overseers. Edwin Epps with over three hundred acres of land did his own overseeing of the work of slaves on his plantation. With 150 to 200 slaves, however, this would not have been possible. The planter himself or an overseer rode into the fields on horseback. Most were armed with pistols. Some carried Bowie-knives. Like Epps, many carried whips. Often the planters or overseers had dogs trotting along with them. These were usually the kind trained to catch runaway slaves.

The planter or overseer kept a sharp lookout over the slaves. His business was to produce large crops. On that the overseer's job depended. The dogs were kept in case a slave attempted to escape. The pistols were there for dangerous emergencies. Pushed to madness by brutal punishment, even a slave sometimes turned on his oppressors. In such cases, a slave had very little chance of surviving. As was true of most of the courthouses in the state, gallows stood on the grounds of the Avoyelles Parish Courthouse in Marksville. A slave was executed there in 1852 for killing his overseer.

The killing happened not far from Epps' plantation. The slave's task had been to cut rails. During the day the overseer sent the slave on an errand. This took so much time he could not finish the task which had been assigned. The overseer told him the errand was no excuse. They were in the back of the woods when the overseer approached the slave. He ordered him to kneel and bare his back for a lashing. The boy submitted to the pain of the overseer's whip until he was insane. Mad with pain, he seized an axe and literally chopped the overseer to pieces.

He made no attempt to hide the act. He went to his master and told him the story. He told him he was ready to die. He was led to the scaffold with the rope around his neck. He showed no fear.

Besides overseers or planters, certain slaves were named drivers. They were compelled to do the whipping of their fellow slaves. They did their own share of the work but had this additional role. They worked with whips around their necks. If they failed to use them as ordered, they themselves were whipped. They received no special privileges for this unwanted part of their jobs.

In cane cutting time slaves were not allowed time to sit down to eat their dinners. Carts were filled with corn cakes cooked in the plantation kitchen. They were taken to the slaves for dinner. It was the duty of the driver to distribute them. They had to be eaten within a brief break from the work.

Platt almost became sick himself when he was a driver of a gang of slaves at Hawkins' plantation. A slave working in the hot sun at the hard labor of cane cutting suddenly fell to the ground. He had become so hot he quit perspiring. He had been taxed beyond his strength. Platt dragged him into the shade of the tall sugarcane. There he threw dashes of water upon him. As soon as the man recovered, he had to return to work.

On Bayou Huffpower when Platt first arrived at Epps' plantation, one of Joseph Robert's Negroes was the driver. His name was Tom. He was a burly fellow who seemed to have little sympathy for his fellow slaves. Platt thought such a job a horrible one. He knew he would never want to be a driver.

Yet when Epps moved to Bayou Boeuf, he made Platt his driver. Platt hated wearing the whip around his neck. If Epps were around, Platt was forced to show no mercy. He was not going to risk getting the whipping himself. This was the penalty for not carrying out the master's orders to whip another slave. Epps took pride in believing that he never missed an offense a slave committed. At night he went to the cabins to locate any slave he had found violating one of his rules. Not only was the slave punished but Platt also if he had permitted it.

On the other hand, if Platt applied the lash freely, Epps was satisfied. Platt worked out a plan to handle the job with less pain for himself and the other slaves. During his eight years as a driver, Platt became very skilled in using his plan. He learned to throw the lash within the width of a hair from a slave's back, ear, or nose without once touching them. If Epps was within earshot, Platt applied the whip vigorously. As agreed upon, the victim would squirm and screech in agony. Not one of them had been grazed. Of course, the success of the plan depended entirely upon how closely Epps watched over the whipping.

If Epps came up, Patsey could be heard mumbling complaints the whole time about Platt lashing the slaves. Uncle Abram would declare roundly he had whipped them more than General Jackson had whipped the enemy. If Epps was not drunk, this all went well. If he was, one or more of the slaves had to suffer. Sometimes his violence assumed a dangerous form. Once the drunk mad man thought it would be fun to cut Platt's throat.

One day Epps had gone to a shooting match at Holmesville. None of the slaves were aware that he had returned. While hoeing beside Patsey, Platt heard her say suddenly in a low voice, "Platt, did you see Hog-Jaw beckon me to come to him?"

Epps was standing at the edge of the field. He was making faces and motions like he did when he was drunk.

Platt whispered to Patsey to keep on hoeing. He told her not to look up. She could make out she had not noticed the signal Epps gave her.

Epps came up to them in a rage. "What did you say to Patsey?" he demanded with a curse. Platt pretended he did not know what he was talking about. Epps became more enraged.

"How long have you owned this d—n plantation, you d—n nigger?" he sneered. He took hold of Platt's shirt collar with one hand, putting the other in his pocket. "Now, I'll cut your throat. That's what I'll do!" He drew the knife from his pocket. But with his one free hand he was unable to open it. Then he caught the blade with his teeth and opened it. Platt knew he had to get away from him. It was clear he was not joking. Platt's shirt was open in front. When he turned around quickly and sprang away from Epps, Epps held even more tightly to the shirt collar. The shirt ripped off Platt's back. Shirtless, Platt ran, and Epps chased him until he was out of breath. He stopped until he could recover. Then he swore loudly and renewed the chase. He commanded Platt to come to him. Then he tried to coax him to come. Platt kept his distance. The two circled the field several times. Epps made several desperate plunges toward Platt. Platt dodged them. By then Platt was more amused than scared. He not only knew Epps could not catch him, but he also knew Epps himself would laugh at his own drunken folly once he became sober.

After awhile, Platt saw Mrs. Epps standing by the yard fence. He ran towards her. He told his story. Epps did not follow this time. Instead he stayed an hour or so in the field. Platt continued to stand by Mary Epps. She became very upset again. She poured out all her anger at Epps and Patsey in a scary recital to which Platt had to listen.

In a short while, they saw Epps coming toward the house. He attempted to look as innocent as a child. The expression on his face was a happy one. His eyes were downcast as though he were thinking of things far away. He walked with his hands behind his back. He was nearly sober.

Mrs. Epps was in no mood to play games. She demanded to know from him why he was trying to cut Platt's throat. She was so angry her face became very red. Her voice was high.

Epps continued his game of pretend. He acted shocked at her anger. He swore by all the saints he had not spoken to Platt all day. "Platt, you lyin' nigger, now have I?" he asked shamelessly.

It was not safe to contradict a master. The truth had nothing to do with it. When Epps went into his house, Platt returned to the field. The incident was never mentioned again.

After such incidents, Platt's thoughts turned desperately to a subject that he had often considered. That was finding a way to get word back to his wife, Anne, regarding his whereabouts.

He wanted badly to write a letter and get it mailed to Saratoga, New York. This was no simple matter at all for a slave. To begin with, he could not allow anybody to know he could read and write. There was a Louisiana law passed in 1830 prohibiting whites from teaching slaves to read and write. Planters were afraid of slaves who could do so. The fear was they might cause trouble for them with other slaves.

Epps had made his feelings on the subject loud and clear to Platt. Soon after Epps purchased Platt, he had asked him if he could read and write. Platt told him he had had a little instruction. He did not ask anything about Platt's past life. Epps replied that if he ever caught him with a book, he would give him a hundred lashes. He said he wanted him to understand that he bought "niggers" to work, not to educate. So there was the fact that a project of writing and mailing a letter had to be secret.

Fig. 31. Northup stole a sheet of paper and used a duck's feather for a quill to write a letter to his home folks to let them know he was held as a slave on Bayou Boeuf.

Mrs. Epps had once asked about his past life. He had simply told her he was from Washington. She assumed he was a native there. More than once Mrs. Epps remarked that he did not talk or act like the other "niggers." Not to her or anyone else had Platt given any hint he could read and write.

There was no way to obtain a sheet of paper, ink, or pen. If he managed to obtain all these and wrote the letter, he could not leave the plantation without permission. He had to have a pass. A postmaster would not mail a letter from a slave without written instructions from his owner.

One winter Epps was in New Orleans. His wife sent Platt to Holmesville to make several small purchases. He had a chance to take a sheet of paper. He stuck it under a board in his cabin.

He tried making ink. He boiled white maple bark. One day he plucked a duck's feather and cut it to make a quill. When the other slaves in the cabin were asleep, Platt wrote his letter. He was lying on his plank couch and writing by the light from the coals in the fireplace.

He wrote to a man in Sandy Hill, New York. He described his condition and asked for help.

For a long time he kept his letter.

One day a man named Armsby came to the plantation. He wanted a job as overseer. He applied to Epps for such a position. Then he went across the bayou to Shaw's. He stayed at Shaw's for a few weeks. Shaw was a man of low character. He was a gambler. His slave, Charlotte, was the mother of a brood of young mulattoes. Shaw was the father of the children who were growing up in his house. It was there Armsby was allowed to visit.

Armsby was without a job or any chances of getting one. He became so desperate that he was forced to work in the fields with the slaves. A white man working in the fields was a rare sight on Bayou Boeuf. A white man who did manual labor was considered low class — almost on the same level as the slaves.

Platt talked with Armsby as they worked side by side in the field, Armsby said he often went to Marksville twenty miles away. By now Platt felt his situation was so hopeless he lost his good judgment. He decided to ask Armsby to mail the letter for him. One night he slipped over to Shaw's and woke Armsby up. He whispered the question about Armsby mailing a letter for him. Platt begged him not to say anything to anybody about his coming there and asking him to do this. Platt told Armsby he had some coins given him for his fiddling and he would give these to him.

No sooner had Platt left Armsby that night than he knew he had made a terrible mistake. It could have been a fatal mistake. From that moment Platt lived miserable with fear. Fortunately, he had not given Armsby the letter. He had told him he would write the letter in a few days. Platt wished with all his heart he had not gone to Shaw's. Most of all he wished he had not confided in Armsby. But this he had done, and he had to live with it. He worried about it night and day. He could not sleep worrying about it.

Later, one day while his slaves were scraping cotton, Epps seated himself on the fence that formed a line between his place and Shaw's. Armsby came and took a seat beside him. Platt watched in agony.

That night Platt was broiling his bacon in his cabin when Epps appeared at the door. He carried his rawhide whip in his hand. "Well, Boy," he said, "I understand I've got a larned nigger. One that writes letters. And tries to get white fellows to mail 'em. Now wonder if you know who that is?"

Platt's worst fears were realized. "Don't know nothin' about it, Master Epps." He assumed an air of ignorance and suprise. "Don't know nothing at all about it, Sir."

"Wasn't you over to Shaw's night before last?" Epps asked.

"No, Master," was the reply.

"Haven't you asked that fellow, Armsby, to mail a letter in Marksville for you?"

"Why, Lord, Master, I never spoke three words to that man in my whole life. I don't know what you mean."

"Well," Epps said, "Armsby told me today the devil was among my niggers. He said I had one needed close watching or he would run away. When I axed him why, he said you come over to Shaw's and waked him up in the night. Said you wanted him to carry a letter to Marksville. What do you got to say to that, huh?"

"All I've got to say to that, Master, is there is no truth in it. How could I write a letter without ink or paper? There is nobody I want to write to 'cause I ain't got no friends living as I knows of. That Armsby is a lying, drunken fellow, they say. Nobody believes him anyway. You know, I always tell the truth and that I never go off the plantation without a pass. Now, master, I can see what that Armsby is after plain enough. Didn't he want you to hire him as an overseer?''

''Yes, he wanted me to hire him.''

''That's it!'' Platt said. ''He wants to make you believe we're all going to run away, and then he thinks you'll hire an overseer to watch us. He just made that story out of whole cloth 'cause he wants to get a situation. It's all a lie, Master. You may depend on't.''

Epps mused awhile on that. ''I'm d—n Platt, if I don't believe you tell the truth. He must take me for a sucker to think that he can come over here with this kind of yarn, mustn't he? Maybe he thinks he can fool me. Maybe he thinks I don't know nothin'. Can't take care of my own niggers, eh? Soft soap old Epps, huh? Ha, ha, ha, ha! D-d Armsby! Set the dogs on him, Platt.'' He commented on Armsby's general character. He vowed he was capable of taking care of his own business. With a remark that he could jolly well attend to his own niggers, Epps left.

When Epps was gone, Platt threw the letter into the fire. With a despairing heart he saw the letter which he had worked so hard to get written disappear into smoke.

Not long after Armsby was driven from Shaw's plantation. Platt was much relieved. He always feared Armsby might renew the conversation. Next time Epps might believe him.

Fig. 32.   Patrols were men named by the police juries of each parish in Loui-siana to police plantation countries at night. It was their duty to see that slaves stayed in their cabins at night and did not visit other plantations.

CHAPTER SIXTEEN

The year 1850 was an unlucky one for Wiley, Platt's fellow slave on Epps' plantation.

Wiley was one of those very quiet, silent "niggers" so far as Epps was concerned. Yet underneath all this he was warmly social and a man of courage. One night, he had the foolhardiness to leave the Epps quarters and visit a neigboring cabin. Of course, he had no pass.

Wiley was enjoying himself so much he forgot how much time was passing. Daybreak came before he suddenly realized what a problem he might have made for himself. He sped home as fast as he could go. He hoped to reach there before the horn blew. It was his bad luck to be seen by a company of patrollers.

On Bayou Boeuf an organization of patrols was on duty at night. Their business was to patrol the roads and lanes of plantation areas by night. They rode on horseback to be sure the slaves were in their cabins. They patrolled with dogs trained to catch runaways. It was their business to seize any slave they found wandering from his home plantation who did not have a pass. They had the right to punish the slave themselves. They could whip him. They could even shoot him if he attempted to escape. These men were appointed by the Avoyelles Parish Police Jury. This was done by police juries in all plantation country.

Each company of patrols had a certain distance to ride up and down the bayou. Each planter contributed to their pay according to the number of slaves owned. If Wiley had not been enjoying himself so much, he would have heard the horses' hoofs clattering along the lanes. These could be heard every hour of the night all night long. Often the patrols could be seen driving a slave ahead of them. Or they led a slave with a rope around his neck back to his master's plantation.

Wiley was brought to reality that morning when he walked plainly in view of some of these patrols. His first thought was to run for his cabin which he hoped to reach before the patrollers could overtake him. But their dogs were unleashed and came rushing at poor Wiley. One of these great hungry dogs gripped him by the leg. The dog held him fast.

When the patrollers came up, they gave Wiley a terrible whipping. After that, they took him as a prisoner to Epps. The cuts of the lash and the bites of the dog left him in misery. Then Epps gave him another whipping. After that, he was scarcely able to move.

Wiley took his place in the field, but he could not keep up. There was not an hour of the day he was not hurting from the two whippings with rawhide.

So great were Wiley's sufferings that he decided he could no longer bear the situation. He would run away. He did not even tell his wife. He made his plans. First he cooked his whole week's allowance of bacon and corn. Then, taking the food with him, one Sunday night he slipped out of the cabin.

The next day when the horn sounded he was not there. A search was made through the cabins. The corn crib and cotton house were searched. He was nowhere to be found. Each slave was asked by Epps to tell what he knew about Wiley. Nobody, not even his wife, knew anything.

Epps raved and stormed. When nothing more could be done on the plantation, he galloped off to ask the neighbors if anybody had seen Wiley. The dogs were led to the swamp. They did not pick up his trail. They circled the woods with their noses to the ground. Always, the dogs returned to the spot from which they had started.

Three weeks went by. All hope was gone of ever seeing Wiley again. Then to everyone's surprise he appeared at Epps' place. He told how he had reached the shore of Red River. While planning how he would get across, a white man appeared. He asked to see Wiley's pass. Of course, Wiley had no pass. He was taken to Alexandria, the parish seat of Rapides Parish. There he was placed in prison.

Several days later Mrs. Epps' uncle, Joseph B. Robert, was in Alexandria. It was Robert who had owned the plantation worked by Epps on Bayou Huff-power. By chance he saw Wiley. Wiley had worked on Robert's plantation. Robert paid the jail fee and wrote a pass. He requested that Epps not whip Wiley on his return. Robert sent him back to Bayou Boeuf.

Epps paid no attention to Robert's request. He had Wiley stripped. Then Wiley had to endure another of Epps' inhuman floggings. This was the first and the last of Wiley's attempts to run away. The long scars on his back would forever remind him of the danger of running away.

Platt, like the other slaves, knew that the woods were filled with runaways.

Once Platt, without knowing it, revealed the hiding place of six to eight slaves hiding in the Great Pine Woods.

Adam Taydem sent Platt from the mills to secure provisions from Ford's place at the opening. The entire distance lay through the virgin pine forest thick with trees.

On a moonlit night he was returning along the Texas Road. He carried a dressed pig in a bag flung over his shoulder. Suddenly there were footsteps behind him. Two black men in the dress of slaves approached him rapidly. One raised a club to strike him. The other snatched the bag from him. He dodged them both. Hurling a pineknot at the head of one of them, he knocked the man senseless. Just then two more appeared on the side of the road. He succeeded in running past them, fleeing as fast as he could. He was scared and never slowed down until he arrived at the mills. There he told his story.

Adam Taydem took action. He aroused Cascalla, the Indian chief, to go with him to the scene of attack. They found a puddle of blood. That came from the man hit with the pine knot. After searching through the woods one of Cascalla's men saw smoke curling up through the pines. The place from where the smoke came was surrounded. A group of runaway slaves was taken prisoners. They had escaped from a plantation near Lamourie three weeks before.

Keary's plantation contained at least 1500 acres and bordered the Epps' plantation. Keary raised sugarcane on the plantation. He also cultivated six hundred acres of corn and cotton. On his plantation there were about 150 adult slaves. There were about the same number of children.

Augustus was a driver on Keary's plantation. With a pleasant disposition Augustus showed an intelligence much beyond that of the ordinary slave. Somehow he angered Keary's overseer. As a result, the overseer beat him mercilessly. Augustus ran away. When he reached Hawkins' place, he hid in a stack of sugarcane.

Dogs — fifteen of them — were sent to track Augustus. They scented his tracks until they came to where he was hidden in the stack of sugarcane. Baying and scratching, the dogs could not reach him. The overseer climbed atop the stack of sugarcane and drew Augustus out. When the slave rolled to the ground, the entire pack of fifteen dogs plunged upon the helpless man. Before they could be beaten off him, the dogs had gnawed and torn his body in shocking manner. Their teeth penetrated to the bone in a hundred places. He was picked up, loaded on a mule, and taken back to his cabin. He died the next day.

Women were often runaways too. Nelly, a slave of Eldred, was one of these. Nelly had worked with Platt in the Big Canebrake. She ran away from Randal Eldred's plantation a mile or so up Bayou Boeuf. She came to Epps' place and hid in his corn crib for three days. At night she stole into the quarters for food. Then she would return to the crib. Finally, Epps' slaves told her they dared not risk helping her any longer. Without this support, she had to return to her cabin.

Among Keary's girls was Celeste. She was around twenty years old and far whiter than her master. It was hard to see any trace of African blood. A stranger would never have dreamed she was a slave.

One night Platt was sitting in his cabin playing his fiddle. Suddenly the door opened. There was Celeste. She was pale and haggard. If a ghost had visited, Platt could not have been more startled. "Who are you?" Platt demanded.

"I'm hungry. Give me some bacon," was her reply.

At first Platt thought this was the insane wife of some planter. He thought she must have wandered from home. Was it his fiddle which had brought her to his cabin? Platt wondered, feeling sick that she had come. She was not black at all. Yet she wore the coarse dress of a slave woman.

"What is your name?" Platt repeated.

"My name is Celeste. I belong to Keary. I've been two days out there among the palmettoes. I am sick and can't work. I'd rather die out there than be whipped to death by the overseer. Keary's dogs won't follow me. They have tried to set them on. There is a secret between the dogs and Celeste. They won't mind the devilish orders of the overseer. Give me some meat. I am starving!"

Platt divided his scanty rations. Then she told him her story of how she had escaped. She described where she was hiding. Not a half mile from Epps' house were thousands of acres of land covered with palmetto. The long arms of tall trees interlocked each other over the place where she was hiding. The trees formed a canopy over it. The cover was so dense that sunbeams did not penetrate. At the heart of this Celeste had made a crude shelter with fallen branches. She had covered it with palmetto leaves.

For several nights she came to Platt's cabin for food. One night Epps' dogs barked. This caused Epps to check out the quarters. Luckily he did not discover Celeste. After that, Platt told her it was not wise for either of them for her to return. Platt agreed to take provisions where she could find them.

Celeste spent the summer in hiding. By fall, terrified by wild animals, she concluded she had no choice. She had to return to Keary's. By then she was healthy and strong. She was whipped. Then she was placed in the stocks. Again she was sent to the fields.

In 1837 a large number of slaves on Bayou Boeuf had formed a movement. In every slave-hut on the bayou the story was told and retold. Platt heard it many times. The leader, Lew Cheney, belonged to Peter Compton on his plantation on Red River. It was this slave who conceived the idea of escape. Slaves along the Boeuf would organize and fight their way to Mexico. Lew Cheney was shrewd. He was very intelligent and full of treachery.

In a remote spot in the swamp behind Hawkins' place the slaves would meet. Lew flitted from plantation to plantation. In the dead of night he preached flight to Mexico. A furor of excitement arose. At length numbers of runaways assembled. They collected supplies over the months. Stolen mules and corn taken from the fields were hidden. Bacon was taken from smokehouses. All was secreted in the woods. Just as the slaves were ready to leave, the plot was revealed. Lew Cheney — the leader of the plot — reported to the planters! Convinced the plot was doomed to fail, he sacrificed his followers. He told the planters that the slaves had planned to murder every white person on the bayou. This filled the country with terror.

The hiding place was raided. Fugitives were taken prisoners. They were taken to Alexandria and hanged. Not only those involved but any slaves suspected were hanged. The whole country was in a state of shock.

Planters finally rebelled at such reckless destruction of property. That did not happen until a regiment of soldiers arrived from some fort on the Texas frontier. The soldiers demolished the gallows. They opened the doors of the Alexandria prison. The slaughter was ended. Lew Cheney escaped. He was paid $500 to enable him to leave the state. He was emancipated by the state legislature in 1838 — the year after the plot was revealed.

Many slaves thought over the matter frequently. There were on-going discussions in the cabins about such things. In the end only certain defeat seemed the result of such attempts. So the idea was always abandoned for the time being.

CHAPTER SEVENTEEN

Wiley suffered severely at the hands of Epps. In this respect he fared no worse than other slaves. Epps was subject to fits of ill humor. On those days — and they were all too frequent — he inflicted punishment on any slave who crossed him. There might be little or no reason at all for Epps to inflict terrible whippings on helpless slaves.

One day a Mr. O'Neal arrived at Epps Plantation from the Great Pine Woods. His object was to buy Platt. The man was a furrier and tanner by trade. He would place Platt at some department of his large business. Aunt Phebe, as cook at the Big House, overheard the talk.

That night Aunt Phebe rushed to meet Platt. She thought to excite him with the news she had just heard. "Massa Epps g'wine sell you to a tanner ober in de Pine Woods." She talked so long and so loud Mrs. Epps overheard her. Platt and Phebe did not know this. Nor did he know Mrs. Epps was listening when he answered her.

"Well," Platt told Aunt Phebe, "I'm glad of it. I am tired of scraping cotton. I'd rather be a tanner. I hope he'll buy me."

O'Neal and Epps did not agree on a price. Therefore, the sale did not come off. The next morning O'Neal left. He was hardly out of sight when Epps came to the field. Nothing so touched the ego of a planter as the idea one of his slaves would like to leave him. This was especially true of Epps. Mrs. Epps had repeated Platt's words to Aunt Phebe. The next morning, as soon as he arrived at the field, Epps headed toward Platt.

"So, Platt, you're tired of scraping cotton, are you? You would like to change your master, eh? You're fond of moving 'round — traveling, ain't ye? Ah, yes — you like to travel. For your health, may be? Feel above cotton scraping, I s'pose. So you're going into the tanning business? Good business — devilish fine business. Enterprising nigger! B'lieve I'll go into that business myself! Down on your knees. Strip that rag off your back! I'll try my hand at tanning!"

"How do you like tanning?" he exclaimed as the rawhide hit the bare flesh. "How do you like tanning?" he repeated with every blow. In this manner he gave Platt twenty or thirty lashes. Over and over he used the word "tanner." When finished "tanning" Platt, Epps allowed the man to get up. With a nasty laugh Epps told him he would give him further "tanning" lessons if he wanted them.

One day Platt returned to the cabin from an errand for Mrs. Epps. There lay Uncle Abram in a pool of blood. He told Platt he had been stabbed. This had happened while he was spreading cotton on the scaffold to dry. Epps came home drunk from Holmesville. He started giving orders to Uncle Abrams. They made no sense. Uncle Abram became confused. With Epps' drunken shouts the slave panicked. He did not know what to do. This enraged Epps. So wild did he become that he flew upon the old man with a knife, stabbing him in the back. The deep cut made a long, ugly wound. Mrs. Epps heard Uncle Abram's cries and went to his help. She sewed the wound. She wept at her husband's cruelty. She declared she expected him to bring their family to poverty. She vowed he would kill all the slaves in his drunken fits.

It was no uncommon thing for Epps to knock Aunt Phebe down with a stick of wood. Yet the worst whipping he ever gave was reserved for Patsey.

One Sunday in hoeing time, the slaves were washing their clothes in the bayou. Patsey was not with them. Epps called loudly for her. There was no answer. No one had seen her leave the yard. In a few hours she was seen returning from Shaw's. Shaw and Epps were not on friendly terms. Shaw's black mistress, Charlotte, knew of Patsey's troubles with Epps. She was especially kind to her. At every chance Patsey found she was in the habit of going to visit Charlotte.

A suspicion entered the brain of Epps. What if she were really going over there to see Shaw? Patsey found her master in a rage when she returned that day. His violence so alarmed her that at first she tried to evade his questions. This only increased his rage. Finally, she drew herself up proudly. In anger she denied the charges.

"Missus don't give me soap to wash with like she does the rest," said Patsey, "and you know why she don't. I went over to Charlotte's to get some soap." She took the soap out of her pocket and showed it to him. "That's what I went to Shaw's for, Master Epps," she went on. "The Lord knows that is all."

"You lie, you black wench," Epps shouted.

"I don't lie, Massa Epps. If you kill me, I'll stick to that."

"Oh, I'll fetch you down. I'll learn you to go to Shaw's. I'll take the starch out of ye."

Epps turned to Platt. He ordered him to drive four stakes into the ground. He pointed with the toe of his boot where he wanted them. When the stakes were driven down, he ordered her to remove all of her clothes. Ropes were brought and the girl was tied firmly to a stake. He went to the gallery and secured a heavy whip. Placing the whip in Platt's hands, he ordered him to lash her. Platt recoiled, but he had to obey. It took the worst of devils to program such a terrible act.

Mrs. Epps stood with her children on the gallery. She watched with heartless satisfaction. The slaves huddled together. Their faces mirrored their horror. Patsey prayed for mercy. Her prayers were in vain. Epps ground his teeth and stamped the ground. He screamed louder and louder at Platt, "Harder!"

"Oh, mercy, Massa! Oh, have mercy, do! Oh, God! Pity me!" Patsey cried over and over. She struggled fruitlessly.

This happened on a Sunday afternoon. This horrible whipping was in contrast to the beauty of the peaceful countryside. The Boeuf plantations were in their glory. The fields smiled in the warm sunlight. A thousand birds sang. The trees were rich in green foliage. Peace and happiness seemed to prevail.

Fig. 33. Platt hated being forced by Edwin Epps to whip Patsey.

But at the Epps plantation there was a horror no-body involved could ever, ever forget.

Platt was told to take the nearly lifeless woman back to her cabin. She could not stand. What voice she had was too faint to be heard. Her dress was replaced.

The slaves laid her on boards in the cabin. At night Aunt Phebe rubbed her wounds with tallow. Day after day Patsey lay on her face in the cabin. The sores prevented her resting in any other position. All of the slaves tried to help and console her.

From that time forward she was never the same. She no longer moved with that bounding and elastic step. There was not that pretty sparkle in her eyes that once set her apart. The laughter-loving spirit of her youth was forever gone. She fell into a depression and became more silent every day. Working with other slaves, she said not a word. A careworn, listless expression settled on her face. She wept often. If ever there was a broken heart, that heart belonged to Patsey.

It was sad for Epps' slaves to see that his young son was growing up to be just like his father. Ten or twelve years old, Edwin was an intelligent boy. He relished playing the master. Especially did he imitate his father in chastising Uncle Abram. He would call the old man to account. If in his childish judgment it was necessary, he sentenced him to a number of lashes. These the child gravely applied. Mounted on his pony, he rode into the fields with a whip. Playing the overseer, he delighted using the rawhide to whip the slaves. He laid the whip on them with loud shouts. Sometimes he cursed. The old man laughed. He praised his son as a regular boy.

Fig. 34. Edwin Epps owned a cotton plantation on Bayou Boeuf.

CHAPTER EIGHTEEN

Mr. Avery, a carpenter from Bayou Rouge, was hired by Edwin Epps to build a house. This was in the year 1852.

Although the home of a planter was called "The Big House," Epps' house was neither very large nor showy. There were four rooms — the two largest being those side by side in front. Each room opened on the front gallery. This made two identical front doors side by side at the center of the gallery. Behind each of the front rooms was a smaller room. A narrow stairway in one of the back rooms led to the attic. Behind the four-roomed house, set slightly apart from it, was a long narrow kitchen.

The house was very well built. Matched cypress boards covered the ceiling and walls. The floors were of the same durable cypress. A gallery spanned the front of the house.

The planks and boards were generally sawed by slaves with whipsaws.

Located fronting Bayou Boeuf, Epps' house was comfortable. Planned so that whatever breezes there were circulated through the house, it was built with tall ceilings meant to lessen the discomfort of the hot summers. At the right of the gallery was a large cistern to supply the family with water.

"Big Houses" of planters did not necessarily refer to the size of the structures. The planter, the final authority on his plantation, lived there. It was this place where all decisions concerning the plantation and its people were made that caused the term "Big Houses" to come into existence.

Since Platt had some experience as a carpenter's assistant, he was taken away from field work altogether. He was assigned to be an assistant to Avery and his workers when they arrived to begin construction of the house. One of these workers was named Bass. He was to become very special to Platt.

Bass was a large man. He was somewhere between forty and fifty years old. When he spoke, it was after much thought. He loved to argue, but he never offended. Nobody on Bayou Boeuf agreed with Bass on either politics or religion. Nor had any man in the Lower Red River Valley ever discussed these subjects with half so much interest as Bass did. Somehow he created amusement rather than displeasure among his hearers. He said he was a bachelor and had no relatives he knew of. For four years he had lived in Marksville. A native of Canada, he had left home in early life. Goodhearted and kind, he was well liked.

One day Bass and Epps got into an argument. Platt, working at planing boards, listened closely. Epps, Avery, Bass, and slaves were at the work on the house that day.

"I tell you what it is, Epps," said Bass. "It is all wrong, Sir. There is no justice or righteousness in it. I wouldn't own a slave if I was as rich as Croesus. There's another humbug — credit. No credit — no debt. Credit leads a man into temptation. Cash down is the only thing that will deliver him from the evil.

But this question of slavery. What right do you have to your niggers when you come down to the point?"

"What right?" Epps laughed. "I bought 'em and paid for 'em."

"Of course, you did. The law says you have the right to hold a nigger. Begging the law's pardon, it lies. Yes, Epps, when the law says that, it's a liar. The truth is not in it. Is everything right because the law allows it? Suppose they'd pass a law taking away your liberty and make you a slave?"

"Oh, that ain't a supposable case," said Epps, still laughing. "Hope you don't compare me to a nigger."

"Well, not exactly," Bass answered gravely. "But I have no acquaintance with any white man in these parts that I consider one whit better than myself. Now, in the sight of God, what is the difference between a white man and a black one?"

"All the difference in the world," replied Epps. "You might as well ask what the difference between a white man and a baboon. Now, I've seen one of them critturs in New Orleans that knowed just about as much as any nigger I've got. You'd call them feller citizens, I s'pose?" Epps laughed at his own wit.

"Look here, Epps. You can't laugh me down in that way. Some men are witty. Some ain't so witty as they think they are. Now let me ask you a question. Are all men free and equal as the Declaration of Independence holds they are?"

"Yes," Epps said. "But all men. Niggers and monkeys ain't," and he broke into a greater laugh than before.

"There are monkeys among white people as well as black, when you come to that," coolly remarked Bass. "I know some white men that use arguments no sensible monkey would. But let that pass. These niggers are human beings. If they don't know as much as their masters, whose fault is it? They are now allowed to know anything. You have books and papers. You can go where you please and gather intelligence in a thousand ways. But your slaves have no privileges. You'd whip one of them if caught reading a book. They are held in bondage generation after generation. They are deprived of mental improvement. Who can expect them to possess much knowledge? If they are not brought down to a level of brute creation, you slaveholders will never be blamed for it. If they are baboons, you and men like you will have to answer for it. There's a sin — a fearful sin — resting on this nation. It will not go unpunished forever. There will be a reckoning day, Epps. It may be sooner or later, but it is coming."

"If you lived among the Yankees in New England," said Epps, "I expect you'd be one of them cursed fanatics that know more than the Constitution. You'd go about peddling clocks and coaxing niggers to run away."

"If I was in New England," returned Bass, "I would be just what I am here. I would say that slavery ought to be abolished. You have no more right to your freedom than Uncle Abram yonder. Talk about black skin and black blood. Why how many slaves are there on this bayou as white as either of us? The whole

system is as absurd as it is cruel. You may own niggers and be hanged. I wouldn't own one for the best
plantation in the state!''

"You like to hear yourself talk, Bass, better than
any man I ever heard. You would argue black was
white, or white was black. Just so somebody would
contradict you. Nothing in this world suits you.''

Epps and Bass argued the subject often. Epps
provoked the argument for the purpose of getting a
laugh. He looked upon Bass as a man ready to say
anything just to hear his own voice. Epps did not take
him seriously.

Bass remained at Epps' plantation all summer.
Almost every other weekend he returned to
Marksville. Platt was cautious now. He had to be, but
he felt he could trust Bass. It was not a slave's place
to speak to a white man except when spoken to.
Nevertheless, Platt did not omit a chance of throwing himself in Bass' way. He tried in every possible
way to get his attention.

One day in early August, Bass and Platt were
at work alone in the house. The other carpenters had
left. Epps was absent in the field. Now, Platt felt, it
was now or never. Bass would be leaving soon. They
were busily at work in the afternoon. Platt stopped
suddenly.

"Master Bass, I want to ask you what part of
the country you come from?''

"Why, Platt, what put that in your head?'' he
answered. "You wouldn't know if I should tell you.''
After a moment or two he added — "I was born in
Canada. Now guess where that is.''

"Oh, I know where Canada is. I have been there myself."

"Yes, I expect you are well acquainted all through that country," Bass laughed in complete disbelief.

"As sure as I live, Master Bass," Platt replied, "I have been there. I have been in Montreal and Kingston, and Queenston, and a great many places in Canada. I have been in New York state too — in Buffalo, Rochester, Albany. I can tell you the names of villages on the Erie Canal and the Champlain Canal."

Bass turned around and looked at Platt for a long time. He didn't say a word.

"How come you here?" he finally asked.

Platt answered, "If justice had been done, I never would have been here."

"Well, how's this?" asked he. "Who are you? You have been in Canada sure enough. I know all those places. How did you happen to get here. Come, tell me all about it."

"I have no friends here I can trust," Platt replied. "I am afraid to tell you — though I don't believe you would tell Master Epps."

Bass assured him he would keep every word secret. He wanted to know more. Platt told him it was a long story. Epps would return shortly. He told Bass if he would see him that night after everybody was asleep, he would tell him. This suited Bass fine. He directed Platt to come into the building where they were working. He would meet him there.

Fig. 35.   Platt and the carpenter, Bass, met secretly at night along the banks of Bayou Boeuf to plan how Platt could regain his freedom.

About midnight all was quiet and still. Platt crept out of his cabin. Silently he entered the unfinished house. Bass was there waiting for him.

Bass repeated again and again that Platt's story was safe with him. So Platt told him his story. Bass questioned him many times. He wanted all of the details. These Platt supplied. When he had finished telling Bass, Platt asked him to write a letter to his friends in the North. He wanted them to know where he was. He asked Bass to have them forward his free papers.

Bass promised to do these things. He then impressed upon Platt the great necessity of strict silence. Between them they planned a line of action.

The next night they met among the high weeds on the bayou bank. They would need light enough for Bass to write. He must get the names and addresses of persons whom he should contact. Platt gave him the names of William Perry, Cephas Parker, and Judge Marvin. All of them were from Saratoga Springs, New York. Platt had been employed by Judge Marvin at the United States Hotel.

Bass reminded Platt he had been gone from New York a long time. "It is so many years since you left Saratoga, all these men may be dead. Or they may have moved."

The two talked for a long time. Platt told Bass about his family. He mentioned the names of his wife and children.

Bass said he was a lonely man. He was a wanderer about the world. Soon he would reach the end. There would be no one to mourn him. What there was left of his life he proposed to work against slavery.

After that, Platt and Bass were careful not to let there be any suspicion the two had any contact. They rarely recognized each other. Bass spoke less about slavery.

After Bass returned to Marksville, he wrote letters. One he directed to the Collector of Customs at New York. Another he sent to Judge Martin. Another went to Parker and Perry jointly.

When he returned from Marksville, he informed Platt of what he had done. They met at midnight.

The letter was:

"Bayou Boeuf, Aug. 15, 1852

"Mr. William Perry or Mr. Cephas Parker

"Gentleman — It has been a long time since I have seen or heard from you, and not knowing if you are living, it is with uncertainty that I write to you, but the necessity of the case must be my excuse.

"Having been born free, just across the river from you, I am certain you must know me, and I am here now a slave. I wish you to obtain free papers for me, and forward them to me at Marksville, La., Parish of Avoyelles, and oblige

"Yours,

"Solomon Northup

"The way I came to be a slave, I was taken sick in Washington City, and was insensible for some time. When I recovered my reason, I was robbed of my free papers, and placed in irons on my way to this State, and have never been able to get anyone to write for me until now; and he that is writing for me runs the risk of his life if detected."

When Bass returned from Marksville, he told Platt what he had done. They continued to meet at midnight to speak to each other. By day there was no sign they knew each other. They only discussed the work at hand. Bass figured it would take two weeks for a letter to reach Saratoga. The same length of time would be required to get an answer. Within six weeks there should be an answer. If there was going to be answer, it should arrive by then.

Bass and Platt discussed what they would do if his free papers came. He would hold them.

No answer had arrived in four weeks. Six, seven, eight weeks passed. Nothing came. Platt stayed in an agony of suspense. Each time Bass visited Marksville Platt's hopes rose and fell. Finally the house was finished. Bass was leaving. Platt almost gave up in despair.

Bass tried to cheer him up. He told him he would continue to work to free him. Platt's freedom, he told him, from then on would be the chief object of his thoughts.

Time passed slowly indeed. Christmas came and went. Platt's mind was constantly occupied. Did the letters get to Saratoga? Were they misdirected? Were they all dead? Was it that the fate of an obscure, unhappy black man was not important to them?

His fellow slaves began to notice the change in Platt. "Are you sick, Platt?" Patsey asked. Uncle Abram, Bob, and Wiley often questioned him on what he was thinking about so hard. Platt would laugh and think of something to get their attention away from him. He kept his thoughts locked closely in his breast.

Fig. 36.   His fellow slaves began to notice the change in Platt, but he kept his thoughts locked closely in his breast.

CHAPTER NINETEEN

Faithful to his word, the day before Christmas, just as it became dark, Bass came riding into the yard.

"How are you?" said Epps, shaking him by the hand. "Glad to see you."

He would not have been very glad had he known why Bass was making his visit.

"Quite well, quite well," Bass said, "Had some business on the bayou. Figured I'd come by and see you. I thought I'd spend the night."

Epps ordered a slave to take charge of his horse. With much talk and jolly laughter they walked to the Big House. Still, Bass managed to signal Platt with his eyes. It was ten o'clock at night before Platt's chores were done, and he went to his cabin. Uncle Abram and Bob shared the cabin with Platt. Platt laid down upon his board and pretended to sleep. When his cabin mates were sound asleep, he stole out the door. He looked for some sign or sound of Bass. There were neither. He waited until long after midnight but Bass did not appear.

Bass had not dared leave the Big House. The next morning would be better, Bass thought. He rose earlier than was his custom. The long ride ahead of him was ample reason for getting up to get an early start.

Platt had figured this out. He too woke early. He roused Uncle Abram an hour earlier than usual. Then he sent him to the Big House to build a fire. At that season of the year this was part of Uncle Abram's routine.

Platt waked Bob up early, too. He told him master would be up before the mules were fed. Bob knew right well what the result of that would be. Bob jumped to his feet. In a twinkling he was off to the horse pasture.

When both were gone, Bass slipped into Platt's cabin. "No letter yet, Platt," he said. Platt felt sick at this news.

"Oh, do write again, Mister Bass," Bass cried. "I will give you names of a great many others I know. Surely they are not all dead. Surely some one will pity me."

"No use," Bass replied. "No use. I have made up my mind to that. I fear the Marksville postmaster will distrust something I've asked for the mail so much. Too uncertain. Too dangerous."

"Then it is all over!" Platt exclaimed. "Oh, my God, how can I end my days here!"

"You are not going to end them here," Bass said, "unless you die very soon. I've thought this matter all over. I've come to a conclusion. There are more ways than one to manage this business. There's a better and surer way than writing letters. I have a job or two on hand. They will be done in April or May. By that time I'll have a good bit of money. Platt, I am going to Saratoga."

Platt could scarcely believe his senses as the words fell from Bass' lips. He repeated to Platt in a way that left no doubt that this was what he was going to do.

"I have lived around here long enough," he went on. "I may as well be one place as another. For a long time I have been thinking of going back to the place where I was born. I'm as tired of slavery as you are. If I can succeed in getting you away from here, it will be a good act that I shall like to think of all my life. And I shall succeed, Platt. I'm bound to do it. Now let me tell you what I want. Epps will be up soon, and it won't do for me to be caught here. There are many men up there around Saratoga and Sandy Hill who know you. Write down their names. I'll make an excuse to come here again during the winter. I'll need to know who to call on when I go up there. Think of all you can. Cheer up! Don't be discouraged! I'm with you, life or death. Goodbye. God bless you." He left the cabin quickly and returned to the Big House.

This was Christmas Day, but Platt's mind was not on Christmas. His mind was on the message Bass had given him.

After breakfast, Epps and Bass walked around the yard. They spoke of the price of cotton and talked about the weather.

"Where do your niggers hold Christmas?" Bass inquired.

"Platt is going to Tanners today. His fiddle is in great demand. They want him at Marshall's Monday. Miss Mary McCoy, on the old Norwood Place, wrote me a note. She wants him to play for her niggers Tuesday."

He's a rather smart boy, ain't he?" Bass asked. "Come here, Platt," he added, looking at Platt as he walked up to them. It was said as though he had never taken notice of Platt before.

"Yes," replied Epps. He took Platt's arm and felt it. "There ain't a bad joint in him. There ain't a boy on the bayou worth more than he is — perfectly sound and no bad tricks. D—n him, he ain't like other niggers. Doesn't look like 'em. I was offered $1700 for him last week."

"And didn't take it?" Bass questioned with an air of disbelief.

"Take it? No! Devilish clear of it. Why, he's a reg'lar genius. Can make a plough beam, wagon tongue — anything, as well as you can. Marshall wanted to put up one of his niggers agin him and raffle for them. I told him I would see the devil have him first!"

"I don't see anything remarkable about him," Bass observed.

"Why, just feel of him now," Epps urged. "You don't see a boy very often put together any closer than he is. He is a thin-skin'd cuss. Won't bear as much whipping as some. But he's got the muscle in him, and no mistake."

Bass felt of Platt. He turned him around, examining him carefully. Meanwhile, Epps was pointing out all of Platt's good points. His visitor appeared to take little interest in the subject. Consequently, it was dropped. Bass soon left. Out of the corner of his eye he gave Platt another sly look as he trotted out of the yard.

When Bass was gone, Platt started for the Tanner's plantation, Tiger Bend. The owner, Ann Martha

Fig. 37. Mary McCoy gave a fine festival for the slaves every year at Christmas time.

Tanner, was a widow who operated her large plantation herself. Now all Platt was thinking about was his fiddle and playing for the Christmas feasts.

Platt spent Sunday in his cabin. On Monday he crossed the bayou to play for Douglas Marshall's slaves. All Epps' slaves went along. On Tuesday it was the old Norwood Place that held its feast. It was on the same side of the bayou as Marshall's plantation.

Miss Mary McCoy owned the Norwood estate. She was a lovely girl in her late teens. She was the beauty and glory of Bayou Boeuf, Platt thought. She owned about one hundred working slaves.

She had a great many house servants. There were yard boys and young children. Her brother-in-law was her general agent. He owned the adjoining plantation.

Mary McCoy was loved by all her slaves. They had good reason to be thankful they had fallen into such gentle hands.

Nowhere on the bayou were there such feasts. The merry making was at its height at Mary McCoy's. Hers was the favorite place to be for a Christmas feast. Nowhere else was there such delicious food. Nowhere else did the slaves hear a voice speak to them so kindly. No one else was so beloved. No one else filled so large a space in the hearts of thousands of slaves as did Mary McCoy.

On Platt's arrival he found two or three hundred people assembled. The table was prepared in a long building which she had had constructed for just that purpose. This was so the slaves would have a place in which to dance. The table was covered with every kind of food the country afforded. It was the rarest of dinners. Roast turkey, pig, chicken, duck, and all kinds of meat were there. There was baked, boiled, and broiled meat. Vacant spaces on the table were filled with tarts, jellies, frosted cakes, and every kind of pie. The young mistress walked around the table smiling. She spoke a kind word to each and every one. She was enjoying herself.

When the dinner was over, the tables were removed to make room for the dancers. Platt tuned his fiddle and struck up a lively air. Some joined in a nimble reel. Others patted and sang their simple melodies. The great room was filled with music mingled with the sound of human voices and the clatter of many feet.

In the evening the mistress returned. She stood in the door a long time watching the dancers. Platt thought she was gorgeous in holiday dress. Her dark hair and eyes stood out in her fair complexion. Her form was slender but commanding. She moved with dignity and grace. As she stood there, dressed in her prettiest, her face beamed. Platt thought he had never looked upon a human being half so beautiful. All slave owners were not monsters like Edwin Epps or Jim Burns, he thought with a sigh. There were not many angels of kindness like Mistress McCoy. And nowhere could there be found a better man than William Ford.

Tuesday concluded the three day holiday. At daybreak on Wednesday morning Platt passed the plantation of William Pearce. The planter hailed Platt, saying he had received a line from Epps. It gave him permission to detain Platt in order that he might play the fiddle for Pearce's slaves that night. It was daylight the next morning when Platt finally returned to Epps' house. Although tired with loss of rest, he was happy with the coins which jingled in his pockets. Whites who enjoyed his music had contributed freely to him.

On Saturday for the first time in years Platt overslept. Coming out of the cabin to find the slaves already in the field, he was frightened. The other slaves had been in the field for fifteen minutes. Platt left his dinner and water gourd and moved as fast as he could. It was not yet sunrise but Epps stood watching on his gallery. He called after Platt that it was a pretty time of day to be getting up. By working hard Platt finished the row before Epps came to the field. That did not make up for oversleeping. Epps ordered him to strip and lie down. He gave him ten or fifteen lashes. Then he inquired if he thought he could get up sometime in the morning. Platt assured him quite positively that he could. With his back stinging with pain, he went back to work.

On Sunday Bass was on Platt's mind. On him hung his future life. His sore back did not help his feelings. He was unhappy and downhearted all day long. By night he felt he could not take this life of a slave any longer.

The next morning was January 3, 1853. The slaves were in the field by daybreak. It was an unusual morning for the Boeuf with a cold, raw wind blowing. Bob, Patsey, and Wiley had their cotton bags about their necks. Epps happened to come into the field without his whip. This was unusual. He swore that the slaves were getting nothing done. He cursed himself for leaving his rawhide and swore he would be back with it. Then, he declared, he would warm them as well. Yes, he would make them all hotter than hell.

He left, and the slaves talked among themselves. They said how hard it was to pick cotton with numb fingers and to have such a man as Epp stand over them. Epps was unreasonable, they said. As they talked, a carriage moved past them toward the Big House.

Looking up, they saw two men walking toward the cotton field.

Fig. 38.   Epps came to the cotton field without his whip. This was unusual.

CHAPTER TWENTY

What the slaves had no way of knowing was that a series of events had been going on which, in time, brought the two strangers to Epps' cotton field where they were working that cold January day.

Bass's letter to Parker and Perry was mailed in Marksville on August 15, 1852. It arrived in Saratoga in early September. Some time earlier Anne had moved to Glen Falls in Warren County. There she was in charge of the kitchen in Carpenter's Hotel. She kept house. However, she lived with her children.

Parker and Perry sent the letter on to Anne without delay. On reading it, the children were very excited. They rushed to a nearby village of Sandy Hill. This was the residence of Henry B. Northup. Northup was a member of the English family who had owned Solomon's grandfather and set Solomon's father free. They asked his advice and assistance.

Henry Northup, a lawyer, found a New York law which provided for the recovery of free citizens from slavery. It was passed May 14, 1840. It was entitled, ''An Act More Effectually To Protect the Free Citizens of this State from Being Kidnapped or Reduced to Slavery.'' It provided for the governor to take measures to restore such a kidnapped slave to freedom. The law authorized him to appoint and employ an agent. He was to furnish his agent with such documents as needed to free the person.

In turn, the agent was to proceed to collect proof of the person's freedom. Then he was to make such journeys and do all necessary to obtain the slave's freedom. All expenses incurred were to be charged to monies to be secured from the legislature.

For Solomon Northup, this meant proving to the governor that he was a citizen of New York and that he was wrongly held in bondage. The first proof was easy. The second rested on the letter Bass had written to Parker and Perry and among the letters sent from the sailing ship, Orleans. The latter letter had been lost.

Documents were collected. These were shown to be true and were signed by Solomon Northup's wife, Anne Northup. With these documents went letters of citizens of Sandy Hill and Fort Edward, New York, which stated that what Anne Northup wrote was true. There were also letters sent by several men to the governor asking that Henry Northup be appointed agent to attempt to free Solomon Northup.

On November, 1852, Henry Northup was appointed agent by the governor. He was employed to take such measures as were needed to free Solomon.

Henry Northup was unable to leave his business to travel to Louisiana until December. On December 14, 1852, he left Sandy Hill, New York. From there he went to Washington. Senator Pierre Soule, Secretary of War Conrad, and Supreme Court Justice Nelson heard the facts in the case. They added their names to the documents Henry Northup had brought with him. These were important since they meant that these high officials of the nation knew these facts regarding Solomon Northup to be true. These officials in Washington also furnished Henry Northup with letters to people in Louisiana who could assist him in his effort to free Solomon from slavery.

Senator Soule took a deep interest in freeing Solomon Northup, known as Platt in the slave country where Edwin Epps' plantation was located. Henry Northup returned to Baltimore, Maryland. From there he went to Pittsburgh, Pennsylvania. He was advised to go directly to New Orleans. However, when the steamboat on which he was riding arrived at the mouth of Red River, he decided not to do that. If Henry Northup had continued to New Orleans, he would not have met Bass. In that case, he would not have found Platt.

Henry Northup left the steamboat on which he had arrived at the mouth of Red River. He stayed overnight at a boarding house. The next day he took passage on the first steamer that arrived which was going up Red River. He found Red River a sluggish, winding stream. The river flowed through a large area with few settlers living along its banks. All he could see from the steamboat were the great forests and swamps where trees stood in water. On January 1, 1853, at 9 a.m. he left the steamboat near Marksville. The village was four miles from the landing on the river where Henry Northup arrived. A hack waited which he hired to take him into Marksville.

Bass' letter was postmarked Marksville so Northup felt this was the place to begin his search. He located a boarding house and rented a room. Then he walked around the village and saw the courthouse. He wanted to locate the office of a lawyer. He found an office marked "John R. Waddill, Lawyer." When he met Waddill, he found the Marksville lawyer was not only a very intelligent man but was much interested in this case. Waddill looked upon such a kidnapper with horror. Slavery itself depended upon good faith in slave sales, he said.

Marksville, although the parish seat, was only a small village. There was a tavern where men of the village liked to meet to talk over a drink. Waddill invited the New York lawyer to go with him to the tavern and meet some of the other men from Marksville.

The New Yorker was surprised at how small the village was. He saw the rope dangling from a high gallows at the courthouse. Cows and hogs wandered around the dirt streets of the little village.

The letter signed by Solomon Northup was written from Bayou Boeuf. But this was a slave, and who knew by what name he was known on the Boeuf? The idea of finding a man named Solomon Northup among thousands of slaves on Bayou Boeuf was mindboggling. Nobody had ever heard that name. Nor did Henry Northup or anyone at Marksville have any idea by what slave name Solomon was known. Edwin Epps himself would not have recognized the name. He would have said — and honestly — that he knew nothing about a slave named Solomon Northup.

There was another problem about knowing only that the letter was written from Bayou Boeuf. Where in the eighty or so miles of the Bayou Boeuf was it written? On which side? The richness of the soil of the Bayou Boeuf was well known. It had attracted many planters. The Boeuf flowed from near Alexandria southeastward for at least eighty crooked miles. There was no information in the letter about where Northup was captive along the Boeuf.

It was finally decided that Henry Northup and Waddill's brother would go to Bayou Boeuf. Their plan was to travel from plantation to plantation for the entire length of the bayou and inquire about such a slave. Waddill provided the use of his carriage for the trip. Henry Northup and Waddill's brother decided to start early on Monday morning.

This effort may well have proven futile. They could never have gone into the fields. Gangs of workers in the fields could not be reached. Planters were suspicious of strangers and would never have allowed them entrance to their plantations. With the growing stories of abolitionists coming from the North no stranger would be allowed to talk to a planter's slaves.

Nevertheless, this was the plan agreed upon. Perhaps, there was no other choice. The search had to begin. After the decision to drive from one end of Bayou Boeuf to the other was made, Henry Northup and Waddill discussed politics. Waddill observed, "I do not understand your politics in New York. I read of 'soft-shells' and 'hard-shells' ... What does that mean?''

Northup, filling his pipe, told of how a dozen of these small political parties began. They each represented one side of any of a number of political issues. "There is another party, too. These are the

Free-Soilers. They are abolitionists. You have seen none of these in Louisiana?''

"Never, but one," Waddill laughed. "We have one abolitionist here in Marksville. He is a strange creature. He preaches as much as any Northern fanatic against slavery. But he is a kind, generous man. He is always on the wrong side of any argument. We laugh a lot with him. He is a carpenter. His name is Bass.''

"Let me see — let me see!" Waddill repeated. It was as though he were talking to himself. "Bayou Boeuf, August 15...post marked August 15. 'He that is writing for me — Where did Bass work last summer?'' Waddill suddenly asked his brother. His brother did not know. However, he went out to ask other people who might know and came back with the fact. "Bass worked somewhere on Bayou Boeuf.''

"He is the man," Waddill said thoughtfully. There was no doubt in his mind now that here was a key to finding Solomon Northup. Waddill brought his hand down hard on the table. "Bass can tell us about Solomon Northup! I'll bet on it!''

Both Waddills searched for Bass in the village, asking if anybody had seen him. No one had. Finally, they found somebody who said they had heard Bass was at the landing on Red River. Waddill and Henry Northup took a carriage and rode out to the landing. Sure enough, they found Bass there. He was ready to board a steamboat and be gone for several weeks.

Young Waddill introduced Henry Northup to the carpenter. Northup asked for just a few moments of Bass' time.

"Mr. Bass," Northup began, "allow me to ask if you were on Bayou Boeuf last August?"

"Yes, sir, I was there in August," was the reply.

"Did you write a letter for a colored man at that place to some gentleman in Saratoga Springs, New York?"

"Excuse me, sir, if I say that is none of your business," answered Bass. This was a dangerous question, and Bass was on guard. He stopped and looked Northup full in the face.

"Perhaps I am too hasty, Mr. Bass. I beg your pardon. But I have come from New York to accomplish the purpose of a letter dated August 15th. It was postmarked in Marksville. Some things led me to believe that you are, perhaps, the man who wrote that letter. I am in search of Solomon Northup. If you know him, I beg you to inform me frankly where he is. I assure you the source of any information you may give me will be kept strictly to myself."

For a long time Bass looked at the man without opening his lips. He seemed to be questioning whether or not this was a trick.

"I have done nothing to be ashamed of. I am the man who wrote the letter. If you have come to rescue Solomon Northup, I am glad to see you," Bass finally said.

"Where did you last see him? Where is he?" Northup inquired.

"I last saw him Christmas — a week ago today. He is the slave of Edwin Epps, a planter on Bayou Boeuf. His place is near Holmesville. He is not known as Solomon Northup. He is called Platt."

The secret was out. The mystery was unraveled. The two men talked long and freely. Bass said he had intended to go North in the spring. Bass described how he came to get involved with Solomon. He gave an account of Solomon Northup's family. And he told the lawyer how Solomon had been kidnapped. Before separating, Bass drew a map of the bayou on a strip of paper with a piece of red chalk. It showed the location of the Epps plantation. He marked the road leading to it.

Legal action was taken immediately on that Saturday night to test Solomon's right to freedom. Solomon was listed as plaintiff. Henry B. Northup was listed as guardian. Edwin Epps was listed as the defendant. Through this action the sheriff was commanded to take the slave into custody. He was to hold the slave in Marksville until a decision could be made in court. The papers were drawn at midnight by the lawyers. It was too late then to obtain the signature of Judge Cushman. Further business had to wait until after the weekend.

Everything went well until Sunday afternoon. By that time the rumor was out that Lawyer Waddill was after one of Old Edwin Epps' slaves. Bass had become scared for his life and left the state. In leaving he left his affairs with a person at the landing. This person had told the whole story of Henry Northup's purpose in coming to Marksville from New York.

Edwin Epps was well known in Marksville. The question then was whether Henry Northup and the sheriff could find Solomon Northup before Epps heard the story.

Waddill went into action. He sent word to Judge Cushman that he had to see him even though it was by then on a Sunday night. The sheriff was told he would be called after midnight to make a long trip. He was told to have his horse ready and to be prepared to go.

As soon after midnight as bail could be arranged, the carriage left Marksville. The judge had signed the papers requiring that the sheriff bring Solomon Northup to Marksville. The sheriff and Henry Northup began their journey in the night.

The lawyers thought that Epps would go to court in an effort to keep the slave. Henry Northup felt it important, therefore, for the sheriff to witness the first meeting of Solomon with his New York friend.

The sheriff and Henry Northup decided that the sheriff would find the slave first. He would ask him a number of questions about his New York background. He would ask him what was his wife's name? How many children did he have? What were their names? He would ask him about different places in New York. This would establish his identity.

The carriage from Marksville arrived at Epps' field at daybreak. The slaves were already at work picking cotton. The men came in sight shortly after Epps had left the field. Henry Northup and the sheriff got out of the carriage. They told the driver to drive on to the Big House. They themselves started walking toward the field where the cotton pickers were busy. The sheriff told the driver he was not to mention the purpose of their visit at all.

Meantime, in the cotton field, the cotton pickers were curious. To see the sheriff and a strange man walking towards them in the cotton field was a shock. They watched the men closely.

The sheriff walked ahead of the stranger. It was a most unusual sight to see strange men approaching slaves in that manner. This was especially unusual since it was so early in the morning. Uncle Abram and Patsey asked what all of the slaves were thinking: what is this? Who are these people? What do they want with us?

Walking up to Bob, the sheriff asked, "Where is this boy they call Platt?"

"Thar he is, Massa," answered Bob, pointing to Platt.

Platt wondered what they could want with him. He looked hard at the sheriff. He knew he had never seen him before.

"Your name is Platt, is it?" the sheriff asked.

"Yes, Master," he responded.

Pointing towards the other man, he asked, "Do you know this man?"

Solomon looked at the other man for the first time. He was so stunned that he could not speak. Images of his home back North, of Anne and his children, and of his parents flashed before him. His voice, when he finally spoke, was clear. "Henry B. Northup! Thank God! Thank God!"

Platt — Solomon — quickly realized why these men were there. He started to move towards the lawyer.

*Fig. 39. Platt recognized Henry Northup from New York and was overcome
with emotion.*

"Stop a moment," the sheriff ordered. "Have you any other name than Platt?"

"Solomon Northup is my name, Master," he said.

"Have you a family?" he wanted to know.

"I had a wife and three children."

"What were their names?"

"Elizabeth, Margaret, and Alonzo."

"And your wife's name before her marriage?"

"Anne Hampton."

"Who married you?"

"Timothy Eddy of Fort Edward."

"Where does that man live?" he asked, pointing to Henry B. Northup.

"He lives in Sandy Hill, Washington County, New York," was the reply.

The sheriff was proceeding to ask more questions. Solomon pushed past him to reach Henry Northup. He grabbed the man with both hands. He could not speak. He was crying.

"Sol," Henry Northup finally said, "I am glad to see you."

Platt — Solomon — tried to answer. Emotion choked his voice. The slaves, watching all this, were stunned. They stood among the cotton stalks watching the scene with their mouths open.

For ten years Platt had lived among them. He was in the fields with them. At night he was in the cabin with them. He bore the same hardships. He ate the same scanty food they ate. He mingled his grief with theirs. They shared the same few joys. Yet not until this hour had they had the slightest suspicion that Platt was not his true name. They knew nothing at all of his history.

Not another word was spoken among the three men — the sheriff, the lawyer, nor Platt — Solomon. For Platt, he simply clung to Henry Northup. It was as though he thought he would wake up and find out all of this was just a dream.

"Throw down that sack," Henry Northup said to him finally. "Your cotton picking days are over. Come with us to the man you live with."

Platt obeyed him. Walking between him and the sheriff, the trio moved towards the Big House. It was not until they had walked some distance that Platt recovered his voice. He asked then if his family were all still living. Northup told him he had seen his wife, Anne, and his daughters, Margaret and Elizabeth. Alonzo was alive. All were well. Solomon's mother had died.

Recovering from some of the excitement, Platt grew faint and weak. He found it difficult to walk. The sheriff took hold of his arm and helped him. As they entered the yard, Epps was questioning the driver of the carriage. That young man was unable to answer any questions. By the time the sheriff and Northup spoke to Epps, he was as shocked and puzzled as the slaves had been.

Epps shook hands with the sheriff. The sheriff introduced him to Henry B. Northup. Epps invited them into the house. At the same time he ordered Platt to bring in some wood for the fire. Platt managed to cut an armful although he found it hard to handle the axe. When he entered the room where the men sat, the table was strewn with papers. From one of them the lawyer from New York, Henry Northup, was reading.

Platt took his time making the fire in the fireplace so he could listen to what was being said. Very slowly he arranged the sticks of wood in the fireplace. He handled the job of building the fire very quietly so he could hear.

Platt heard the words "the said Solomon Northup" and "Free citizen of New York" repeated. From this the secret Platt had kept from Master and Mistress Epps was now being revealed. He lingered over the fire as long as he dared. When he was leaving the room, Epps asked him, "Platt, do you know this gentleman?"

"Yes, Master," he replied. "I have known him as long as I can remember."

"Where does he live?"

"He lives in New York."

"Did you ever live there?"

"Yes, Master — born and bred there."

"You was born free then. Now you d—n nigger," he exclaimed loudly, "why did you not tell me that when I bought you?"

"Master Epps," Platt spoke in a tone different from what Epps was used to hearing from him, "Master Epps, you did not take the trouble to ask me. Besides, I told one of my owners — the man who kidnapped me — that I was a free man, and I was nearly whipped to death for it."

"It seems there has been a letter written for you by somebody. Now who is it?" he demanded with the ring of his old authority over the slave.

Platt did not reply.

"I say, who wrote that letter?" he demanded again.

"Perhaps I wrote it myself," Platt said in reply.

"You haven't been to Marksville postoffice and back before light. I know."

Epps insisted that Platt tell who wrote the letter. Platt insisted he would not. Epps made many threats against the man — whoever he was. His whole attitude was anger towards the unknown person who had written the letter. He was angry at losing his property.

Epps told Northup if he had only had an hour's notice he would have saved him the trouble of taking Platt back to New York. He would have run him into the swamp or some place out of the way. Then all of the sheriffs in the world could never have found what became of him.

Platt walked out into the yard. He was entering the kitchen when something struck him in the back. It was Aunt Phebe. She was coming from the Big House with a pan of potatoes. She had thrown one hard at Platt. That was her way of letting him know she wanted to speak to him alone.

"Lord a'mity, Platt! What d'ye think? Dem two men come after you. Heard 'em tell Massa you free — got a wife and three children back thar where you come from. Goin' wid 'em? Fool if you don't! Wish I could go!"

Fig. 40. Platt rode away in the carriage to Marksville with Henry B. Northup and the sheriff. A slave was the driver.

Mistress Epps came into the kitchen. She said many things to Platt. She wondered why he had not told her who he was. She said she had rather lose any slave on the plantation than him. She was actually near tears.

Epps had called to Bob to bring up his saddle horse. The other slaves for the moment forgot the penalty for leaving the cotton picking. They were all in the yard. Being still aware, however, they stood behind the cabins out of sight of Epps. They beckoned Platt to come to them. Suddenly he had become a person of great importance.

The legal papers were served. They were read, as the law demanded, to Edwin Epps. Arrangements were made with Epps for him to meet them the next day in court in Marksville.

After this, Henry Northup and the sheriff climbed into the carriage. Platt climbed up to the seat beside the driver.

The sheriff told him that he ought to tell Mr. and Mrs. Epps goodbye. Platt got down from the carriage and ran back to the gallery where both Mr. and Mrs. Epps were standing. He spoke first to Mrs. Epps. "Goodbye, Missus."

"Goodbye, Platt," she said kindly.

"Goodbye, Master."

"Ah, you d—n nigger," Epps muttered in an ugly tone, "you needn't feel so cussed tickled. You ain't gone yet. I'll see about this business in Marksville tomorrow."

Platt had to struggle with himself to be calm. In Epps' eyes he was only a "nigger" who had been taught his place. Yet Platt would have loved to have given Epps a parting kick. On his way back to the carriage, Patsey came up to him. She threw her arms around his neck.

"Oh, Platt," she cried, tears streaming down her face, "you're going to be free! You're goin' way off yonder where we'll never see you any more. You have saved me from a lot of whippings, Platt. I'm glad you are going to be free. But, oh, de Lord, de Lord, Platt! What is going to become of me!"

Platt pulled away from her. He had to be on his way. The driver cracked his whip. Away they went. Platt looked back and saw Patsey with drooping head. The other slaves stood by the gate looking after him. Platt waved his hand. The carriage turned a bend of the bayou, hiding them forever from Platt's eyes.

The carriage stopped a moment at Keary's Sugar House. There a great number of slaves were at work. Henry Northup thought the sugar mill a curiosity. He wanted to see what it was like. While they were stopped, Edwin Epps dashed past them on his horse. He was on his way to the Great Pine Woods to see William Ford. He thought he might learn something from the man who had brought Platt into the Boeuf country.

On January 4, 1853, Epps and his lawyer were in Marksville. His lawyer was H. Taylor. Northup and Waddill met with them. So did the sheriff and Henry Northup. The New York lawyer stated the facts regarding Solomon Northup. He presented the documents supporting these facts. With these was his commission from the governor of New York.

*Fig. 41.   At the Avoyelles Parish Courthouse in Marksville, Louisiana, a
paper was drawn up and signed by all which stated that Northup was a free
man.*

The sheriff told of the scene in the cotton field.

Solomon Northup himself was questioned at length. Finally, Taylor told Epps he was satisfied these were the facts. He told him further legal action would be fruitless.

A paper was drawn up and signed by all. Epps stated he was satisfied that Platt had a right to his freedom. He formally surrendered Platt to the New York agent who represented the Governor of New York Washington Hunt.

Northup and Platt were soon aboard a steamer floating down Red River. Platt — Solomon Northup — was again a free man. He was headed home.

CHAPTER TWENTY-ONE

When they reached New Orleans, Solomon pointed out the location of Freeman's slave pen. He showed Northup the room where Ford purchased him. They learned that Freeman had become a low, miserable rowdy — a broken man.

They visited Genois, the man to whom Senator Soule's letter was directed. They found a man well deserving of his honorable reputation. He furnished Henry and Solomon Northup with a sort of legal pass. It bore his signature and seal of office.

"State of Louisiana,

"City of New Orleans

"Recorder's Office,

"Second District

"To all to whom these presents shall come:

"This is to certify that Henry B. Northup, Esquire, of the County of Washington, New York, has produced before me evidence of the freedom of Solomon, a mulatto man, aged about forty-two years, five feet seven inches and six lines, wooly hair, and chestnut eyes, who is a native of the State of New York. That the said Northup, being about bringing the said Solomon to his native place, through the southern routes, the civil authorities are requested to let the aforesaid colored man Solomon pass unmolested, he demeaning well and properly.

"Given under my hand and the seal of the City of New Orleans this 7th day of January, 1853, "Th. Genois, Recorder."

On January 8, the travelers left by railroad for Charleston, South Carolina. There, boarding a steamboat, they were ready to leave on the final lap of their journey. Henry B. Northup was asked why he had not registered his servant. He replied he had no servant. He had with him a free citizen of New York he had released from slavery.

It seemed the local officials meant to cause him all of the problems they could. After much discussion, Henry and Solomon Northup were allowed to continue their homeward journey.

On January 17, 1853, Solomon Northup caught a glimpse of Goodin's slave pen in Washington. Both of his kidnappers — Birch and Radburn — lived in the city.

It was, of course, necessary to file kidnapping charges against these men. This was done by Henry B. Northup. Birch was arrested but was let out of jail on bond. A former partner of his, Benjamin O. Shekels, posted his bond, meaning that the partner placed the necessary money ($3,000 in this case) by which he promised the prisoner would appear in court when told to do so.

The court proceedings were held on January 18th in the morning. Henry B. Northup had others in court to testify regarding Solomon Northup's life before being kidnapped. General Orville Clark of Sandy Hill, New York, stated that he had known Solomon since he was a child. He said that Solomon was free, as his father had been before him. Henry Northup gave the same information.

Radburn, 48 years old, spoke on behalf of Birch. He said he had known Birch for fourteen years. He said that Birch was keeper of Williams Slave Pen in 1841. He admitted that Solomon had been placed in the pen by Birch in 1841.

When Benjamin Shekels gave his testimony, he said he had been operator of the Steamboat Hotel in Washington in 1841. This was where Birch and Radburn had taken Solomon. Shehels said that they had this slave for sale and gave his history. One of them was the boy's master, Shekel said. They had brought him from Georgia, and he remembered how the slave had wept at their selling him. But, he said, Solomon had said that his master had a right to sell him, the reason being his master had been on a gambling spree!

Solomon was told, Shekels said, that if Birch bought him, he would be sold South. Solomon had answered he had no objections to that. Before 1838, Radburn and Birch had been partners. After 1838, Birch had been a partner of Theophilus Freeman in New Orleans.

Solomon Northup was offered as his own witness. This was denied because he was a Negro. A Negro, at that time, could not give evidence in court.

No Bill of Sale was produced by Birch. A police officer was sent to his house to bring his book with a list of sales for 1841. The sale of Solomon Northup was not listed. Because of the lack of the Bill of Sale, the court ruled that Birch had come to own Solomon innocently and honestly!

Birch actually tried to sue Solomon Northup. He stated that Solomon had worked with his kidnappers

Fig. 42. Solomon and Anne Northup were together after twelve long years.

to defraud him! When the lawyer for Solomon Northup appeared to defend him, Birch asked that he be allowed to withdraw his suit. This he was allowed to do. Birch was cleared of all charges against him.

On January 20, Henry and Solomon Northup left for New York. They arrived in Sandy Hill the next day. Solomon continued the next day to Glen Falls where Anne and their daughters were waiting to see him. Alonzo, their son, lived in the western part of the state. Not long before his father's arrival, Alonzo had written his mother that he wanted to save enough money to buy his father's freedom.

While they waited for Solomon to return, they thought of all that had gone on during the twelve years he had been gone. They had known he had been kidnapped and was a slave somewhere in the South. This they had learned from the letter they received from the sailing ship, Orleans. Clem Ray had also told them about that experience.

There was the day that Margaret and Elizabeth had returned from school in great distress. They were weeping bitterly. In their school books they had seen a picture of slaves in a cotton field. They saw the overseer there with his whip. They worried that this was what their father was enduring. Although they really did not know, this was exactly what was happening to their father at Edwin Epps' plantation.

But, oh, how all those years melted away when Solomon walked in the door of their home! He and Anne held each other close for what seemed a long time to Margaret and Elizabeth. They were all crying now — but this time these were happy tears!

NORTHUP'S JOURNEY FROM
SARATOGA SPRINGS TO LOUISIANA

EDITOR'S NOTES

Slaves were valuable property, and there were not enough slaves to meet the demands of planters with huge acreages in cotton, sugarcane, rice, or tobacco to sell on the world market. By the United States Constitution no slaves could be imported from abroad after 1808. Since slaves could be readily sold for high prices, a number of free persons, like Northup, were kidnapped.

The kidnappers and owners of slave auction barns in Washington, D. C. and New Orleans had an agreement in which they handled such delicate (and illegal) situations as buying and selling a kidnapped slave. This fact gleaned from Northup's account suggests a conspiracy of a group of people from North to South whose object was to kidnap Free People of Color, like Northup, and sell them into slavery.

Immediately after Northup returned to New York, an editor paid him $3500 for the story. It is known that this was done immediately after Northup arrived in New York, since the book was published in 1853, the same year Northup returned. The New York editor, David Wilson, did the research to document all facts relating to Northup's experience in the North, and he interviewed everybody who could add anything to this part of the story. Wilson owned a printing press and had published another book earlier.

Twelve Years a Slave is an account of what slavery was like from one who was there. While Northup's is not the only firsthand account of the slave experience which we have, it is certainly one of the best, if not the best. One of the several mind-boggling aspects of this story is that Northup recalled with such detail the facts of twelve years of life in a country strange to him and a people unknown. Remember that, as a slave, he had no pen nor paper. He wrote down not a single line of his memories. All this experience he recounted to the editor was stored in his head. A keen observer and an intelligent man is reflected in this rare feat. That Solomon Northup and his editor could record the most significant experiences of his twelve years of slavery so that they are clear and probably as objective as could be obtained under the circumstances is a fine achievement for both of them.

Northup's twelve years as a slave on plantations on Bayou Boeuf were spent in the central part of Louisiana which lies in the lower Red River Valley. At the time when Northup lived there, this was remote and isolated country. It was, in fact, on the edge of the western frontier. Miles and miles of pine forests lay between the Bayou Boeuf plantations and the Sabine River, the boundary line between Louisiana and Texas. For long distance transportation settlers depended largely upon steamboat water. Local travel was by foot, horse, or mule, horse or ox-drawn vehicle.

The fact that Solomon Northup had grown up free enabled him to have a viewpoint that persons born slaves could not have enjoyed. He could compare what it meant to be free with the harsh reality of being a slave. As a child of free parents, Solomon attended school. He could read and write. He knew something of geography and the nation's history. He knew something about how the government of the United States worked. These things provided him with far more insight into plantation and slave life than an ordinary slave who had not had these advantages.

By Louisiana Law of 1830 it was illegal to teach a slave to read or write. Planters were always afraid of their slave workers on the cotton and sugarcane plantations. Solomon Northup could not allow his master to discover that he could read and write. A slave could not mail a letter without permission of his master. In fact, he could not leave the plantation without permission of his master.

For Solomon Northup his location in such a remote area on the frontier was an especially distressing fact. Under such conditions in which he lived as a slave and in a country so far away from his home, it took him twelve years finally to get word back to his family where he could be found. Even so, only a combination of the assistance of certain people and sheer luck resulted in his eventual release from slavery.

The experience of one slave was not the same as that of the more than four million slaves on plantations in southern United States. But it is one. Furthermore, every person's name and every place has been checked to see if these people actually existed, as Northup said. The places have been located. Each event, such as a slave uprising of 1837, that could be checked has been found to be an accurate statement of fact. The facts surrounding the kidnapping and persons involved were found in the courts to have been accurate. Whether or not Northup or his editor added, or subtracted, to the story in such things as whippings there is no way of knowing. However, judged by the accuracy of all that was checked and found true, it would seem the book reveals an amazingly factual story of the slave experience.

By the 1850's abolitionists — those who wanted to do away with slavery — were fast bringing the nation to a point of decision about slavery. By 1853 when Northup's book was first published the Civil War was only eight years away. *Uncle Tom's Cabin* by Harriet Beecher Stowe was published the year before and sold millions of copies. *Uncle Tom's Cabin* was fiction. Northup's story was fact. Within a month's time Northup's book sold eight thousand copies. It continued to sell well. There were numerous printings before the war. Four years after the Civil War ended, 1869, the book was published again. It was almost exactly a century later that this editor and Joseph Logsdon co-edited a new edition of the book.

Present Editor, Bayou Boeuf Native

The present editor was born on the banks of Bayou Boeuf on Williamsburg Plantation, located about four and a half miles north of Cheneyville, to a family who were the tenth generation of southern planters. My parents moved across the Boeuf from Williamsburg Plantation to Compromise Plantation when I was two years old. This was shortly after World War 1, and so little had changed in Bayou Boeuf country that Northup would have had little trouble in recognizing his old haunts. There were no slaves, but thousands of black sharecroppers remained in the cabins of nearly countless plantation quarters along the bayou.

When I was about twelve years old, I saw my first copy of *Solomon Northup's Twelve Years A Slave 1841-1853*. It seemed to me the names of all the families of our plantation country were there in print in the Northup book! I had no idea, of course, that my search for every place or person in central Louisiana who had any connection with the book would extend over many decades of my life. Few people of the area even knew of the book; this was no surprise. So confined to earning a living along the bayou were all people, black and white, that they had no time for anything else. The routine of planting cotton, cultivating, harvesting, and selling it went side by side with the cultivation of sugarcane and its harvest and marketing. During the Great Depression time spent on anything but something that contributed to a livelihood for a family was considered lost.

My first copy of the nineteenth century book was purchased in 1936. This was the year I was a freshman at Louisiana State University in Baton Rouge, Louisiana. The book dealer from whom I bought the copy for thirty-seven cents told me emphatically there was nothing to it. It was just another phony story written by abolitionists and never happened. Years later in 1962, in graduate school, I selected the book as a project on which to add more research.

From the time I first read the book until the L.S.U. Press in 1968 published *Twelve Years A Slave* edited by Dr. Joseph Logsdon and me, Dr. Sue Eakin, I tried from time to time to identify this person and that in these two parishes. Nor, indeed, have I ever quit trying to find more information to document Northup's story. It is a continuing search.

The Search for the Truth

What was done to find out if Northup's account was accurate? What sources were found? Where are some of the places visited? How many years did it take?

Dr. Joseph Logsdon concentrated mostly on the business of the trial of the kidnappers and the New York research while I was concerned primarily with Northup's Louisiana experience.

To begin with, Dr. Logsdon spent the summer in New York doing research on Northup's life in New York. He made checks of sources in the Orleans Parish Courthouse, books, U. S. Census records, newspapers, and any archival records he could find.

My concern was to document Solomon Northup's twelve years in Rapides and Avoyelles Parishes. While my childhood was spent in Rapides Parish, I moved to Avoyelles Parish in 1944. This is the parish where Solomon Northup lived ten of the twelve years he was a slave. It was from the Avoyelles Parish Courthouse that he was freed. The sheriff, Judge Cushman, and Lawyer Waddill, along with other individuals involved, lived in Marksville, the seat of government in Avoyelles Parish.

It would be impossible to recount all of the endless miles of driving, the many days spent reading documents in departments of archives, the hours spent telephoning descendants of people mentioned in Northup's book, and the time spent getting old photographs copied.

Here are a few examples of how I came to know that the facts that could be checked in Northup's story are true. William Prince Ford left generations of descendants. One Ford girl was in my classes at Lecompte High School. Lecompte is no more than a mile away from the Great Pine Woods. Indian Creek was a part of our world. Walter Prince Ford, son of William Prince Ford, was mayor of Cheneyville in the early 20th century. A member of the family, hearing

I was trying to find out about an ancestor, sent me photographs of the mayor and his wife. Another relative pointed out the grave of William Prince Ford — unmarked — among a number of other Ford family graves in the Old Cheney cemetery at Cheneyville.

Peter Tanner, who read the Bible to his slaves on Sunday, left many tracks. He left many descendants, and at one time and another I enjoyed talking with a number of them about their ancestor. In doing research on another project, I read personal letters in which Peter Tanner with his hearty laugh was included. At Ezra Bennett's store across the Boeuf from Peter Tanner's plantation he charged items which are listed in surviving ledgers. I found a letter the planter wrote to Louisiana State Seminary regarding his son, Sidney, a student there. In time I found Peter Tanner had moved to a nearby community, Evergreen, and become an early member of Bayou Rouge Baptist Church. There is his grave, with his wife's grave beside it, in Bayou Rouge Baptist Church cemetery.

The clerk of court in Avoyelles Parish showed me the documents of the trial in which Solomon Northup was freed. Judge Cushman's photograph, along with those of all past judges, hangs in the court room at Marksville.

Mrs. Elizabeth Overton Brazelton telephoned me one day to say her great grandfather was Waddill. She had his diary. There were the fabulous pages from that diary; the answer to what happened to Bass, who played such a large role in Northup obtaining his freedom; and Lawyer Waddill's terse notation that he collected fifty dollars for his services from New York lawyer, Henry B. Northup. (Bass died about two months after Northup was freed.)

Mary Dunwoody McCoy had such a magnetic personality that many a letter found in archives mentioned her. The house she was given as a bride still stands. Lucile Bubenzer Schmidt allowed me to copy the photograph of the house where the slave festivals were held. (The house burned sometime in early twentieth century). To my complete delight a student of mine, related to the family, contacted the elderly granddaughter of Mary McCoy, Mary Dunwoody McCoy Wier, in Washington, D. C. Mrs. Wier wrote me wonderful letters about her grandmother. Another granddaughter, who lived in Bunkie, supplied her photograph. The cabin in which her slave lived, the one who stayed close to her after Emancipation, remains standing. Someone supplied a photograph of the slave.

There were many exciting places where I found mention of Mary McCoy. Her grave lies on the banks of Bayou Boeuf near Trinity Episcopal Church at Cheneyville.

Doing research like this is like hunting buried treasure. Surely, the same thrill comes when the treasure is found. In research there is not the glitter of gold, but the find could hardly be more satisfying! Such was the case with the identification of the houses of Edwin Epps. The house he rented from Mary Robert's uncle, Joseph B. Robert, on Bayou Huffpower stands today a few miles from Bunkie, Louisiana. It is called Hillcrest and in 1990 is owned by Mr. and Mrs. J. B. Luke.

The house Edwin Epps built was the biggest treasure to be found. The planter's house there on the Bayou Boeuf was located three miles south of Bunkie and remained much as Epps had left it. It was standing on Bayou Boeuf in what local people called "the bell field" because of the bell shape of the land formed by the bayou. An engineer, father of a next door neighbor in 1944, had lived in the house. So, oddly enough, had a great uncle of mine, one Monroe Lyles!

The Edwin Epps house was moved to Bunkie by a committee of interested citizens. This was after Louisiana State University Press republished the book edited by Logsdon and me in 1968. The museum we still hope to see completed has suffered from lack of any funds with which to make it available to the public. When funds are available, it is hoped that the Epps house will become a museum open to the public, appearing throughout much as it was when the Epps family lived there.

A great-great grandson of Edwin and Mary Epps visited the house of his ancestor. He brought his family with him. Edwin Epps' sons moved to Texas, and there are many descendants there. The twentieth-century Epps couple brought a gift to the Epps house of a picture of the detached kitchen which had burned. They also brought a chart of all of Edwin Epps' descendants!

The United States Census, local cemeteries where the graves of each of the principals have been located, the Avoyelles Parish Courthouse where any number of records document the story, the Avoyelles Parish Police Jury Minutes which include a notation that Edwin Epps was named as a patroller— all of these helped prove that the Northup story is true.

Shared Plantation Life

One of the most important ways I realized that this was a true story came from my own long lifetime spent in exactly the same places Northup spent those twelve years on Bayou Boeuf.

Born and reared on a plantation and studying about them all these years, I can imagine the entire story Northup told as he lived it in this same setting. Plantations did not change in character much from Northup's time until my own. One prospective movie producer came to look at Northup country with a view to making a movie at this location. I'll not forget the day he gasped, lost for how to say what was on his mind. Finally, he shook his head and said," This is like being at a Wake ... It all looks so natural!"

Our movie was never made. A group who had nothing to do with this research, from another section of the country, used the name of the book and made a picture in Georgia. That was the only connection their movie had with the real story — the one we researchers have worked so hard to present to the public *to tell it like it was*! Hopefully, a movie based on the book and filmed in Northup country will some day be made with the same accuracy in telling the story that Northup and his editor used.

In the meantime, the Louisiana Endowment for the Humanities made two grants which provided for marking the Northup Trail with twenty-five permanent markers.

Always it should be noted that the story, as Northup told it after twelve years as a slave, was told without bitterness. Both he and the editor did an unusually fine job. This way we have a slice of history. Remember that Northup, like any historian, had the power of selecting what he wanted to tell — and what he did not. There are some things not included. At least, we have to assume there were many details left out. For instance, were there no slave children other than Edward on Epps' place? Did Bob, Edward, and Patsey not have any children? (They were of childbearing age).

In Northup's personal life, what would you ask if you could review his life with him? Did he dance

— or only play the fiddle at the dances? Were the cabins cold in winter? Couldn't he make himself a pillow out of cotton — or something? Did Epps never issue anything at all but bacon and corn cake? Was it cake? Or cornbread? Did they use the cornmeal to make cush-cush, a popular dish of this area made with cornmeal? Did he catch coons? Enjoy the wild plums, blackberries, dewberries, mayhaws? Didn't Aunt Phebe or Patsey or Solomon make gumbo with 'possums or coons?

There was a lot of good food at the frontier ready for the taking. It is hard to believe that people as intelligent as Epps' slaves did not cook such foods over the fire in their fireplaces. Many — perhaps most — families of whites at that time did not own stoves. Most cooked food over fires in mud fireplaces. Potatoes were roasted in the ashes. Corn was popped. And there was much good food that did not require cooking that would not have needed anybody's permission to pluck off a tree or take from a berry-loaded bush. It was just *there!*

It is interesting to know about the customs which existed in the slave society of which Northup writes. One such custom is the way slaves received their surnames. Slaves were called by the names of their masters, as, for instance, Sam Marshall was a slave named Sam who was from Marshall's plantation, and Harry Keary was from the Keary plantation. These last names of slaves changed when they were sold, each time taking the name of the new owner.

After Emancipation, some discarded these names of their masters, others retained them.

Such details would have made the story fit more perfectly into life as we have known it. We suspect this was, perhaps, not intentionally left out on the part of Solomon Northup. This was the kind of thing nobody would have thought unusual. The editor would not have known to ask.

In any case, Northup's story is as accurate a picture of what life for a slave was like in the Deep South as we are going to get.

Sue Eakin

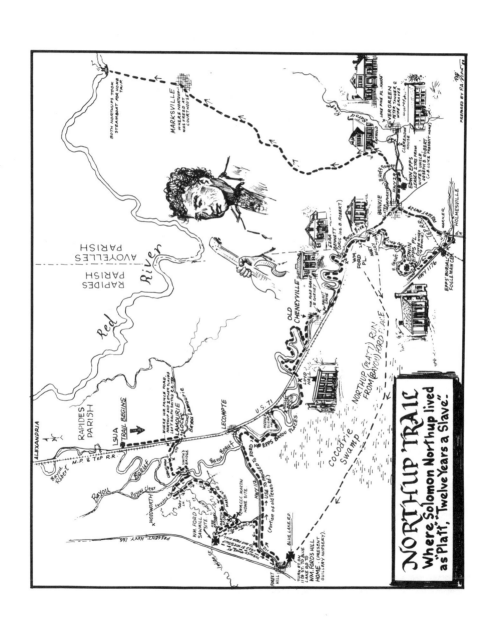

NORTHUP TRAIL

Where Solomon Northup lived as "Platt," "Twelve Years a Slave."

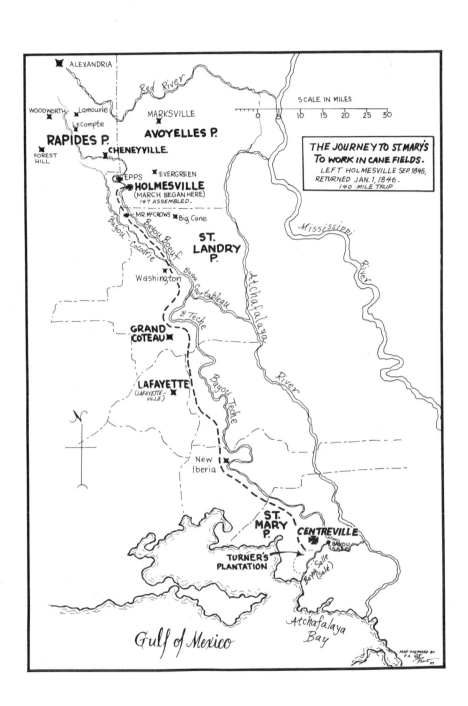

SCALE IN MILES

0   10   15   20   25   30

THE JOURNEY TO ST. MARY'S
TO WORK IN CANE FIELDS.
LEFT HOLMESVILLE SEP. 1845,
RETURNED JAN. 1, 1846.
140·MILE TRIP.

ALEXANDRIA

Red River

WOODWORTH   Lamourie
LeCompte   MARKSVILLE

RAPIDES P.   AVOYELLES P.

FOREST   CHENEYVILLE
HILL

EPPS   EVERGREEN
HOLMESVILLE
(MARCH BEGAN HERE)
147 ASSEMBLED.

MR. M^cCROWS   Big Cane

Bayou Boeuf   ST.
Bayou Cocodrie   LANDRY
                    P.

Mississippi

Washington   Bayou Curtableau

                        Atchafalaya

3 Teche

GRAND
COTEAU

                    River

LAFAYETTE
(LAFAYETTE –
VILLE)

Bayou Teche

N

New
Iberia

                ST.
                MARY   CENTREVILLE
                P.
                            BAYOU
TURNER'S   SALE?
PLANTATION   Bayou Salle (Salé)

Gulf of Mexico   Atchafalaya
                    Bay

MAP PREPARED BY
P.A. PEALE
49